IN THE
SHADOW
OF THE
MOON

AMERICA, RUSSIA, AND THE HIDDEN
HISTORY OF THE SPACE RACE

IN THE SHADOW OF THE MOON

AMERICA, RUSSIA, AND THE HIDDEN HISTORY OF THE SPACE RACE

AMY CHERRIX

BALZER + BRAY

An Imprint of HarperCollins Publishers

Photograph credits: Page 5: © Deutsches Museum, Munich, archives, R0158-01; pages 7, 17, 65, 72, 135: © US Space & Rocket Center; page 18: Everett Collection Inc/Alamy Stock Photo; pages 25 and 83: Photos by Amy Cherrix; pages 34, 78, 138, 157: Bettmann/Getty Images; page 39: Heritage Image Partnership Ltd/Alamy Stock Photo; pages 45, 129, 225: Sputnik/Alamy Stock Photo; page 48: Universal History Archive/UIG via Getty images; pages 66, 133, 253, 261: NASA/MSFC; page 85: Photo by Ernest C. Smartt/Image courtesy of Huntsville-Madison County Public Library; page 91: Universal Images Group North America LLC/Alamy Stock Photo; pages 92, 119, 179: ITAR-TASS News Agency/Alamy Stock Photo; pages 95, 136, 171, 184, 202, 213, 228, 239: NASA; page 97: [Petition for Naturalization of Wernher von Braun, May 10, 1950; Petitions for Naturalization, 1909–1963; Records of the U.S. District Courts (Birmingham, Alabama), Record Group 21]/National Archives at Atlanta; page 142: NASA/JPL-Caltech; page 154: Ralph Morse/Getty Images; pages 196 and 242: Sovfoto/Getty Images; page 201: NASA (HQ # 63-Admin-60); page 211: Central Press/Getty Images; page 272: Collection of Asif Siddiqi; Cover Reference (Korolev): Sputnik/Alamy Stock Photo; Cover reference (von Braun): Imago History Collection/Alamy Stock Photo.

Balzer + Bray is an imprint of HarperCollins Publishers.

Library of Congress Control Number: 2020949242
ISBN 978-0-06-288875-4

Typography by Michelle Gengaro
20 21 22 23 24   PC/LSCH   10 9 8 7 6 5 4 3 2 1
❖
First Edition

This book is dedicated to the memory of those who suffered and died under fascism and to the future generations who must stand vigilant against its resurgences.

CONTENTS

STAGE III: THE QUEST FOR THE MOON

For every action, there is an equal
and opposite reaction.

—Newton's Third Law of Motion

It is the very error of the moon.
She comes more nearer earth than she was wont
And makes men mad.

—William Shakespeare, *Othello*: Act 5, Scene 2

NOTE TO A RELUCTANT READER

If you've picked up this book, chances are you've heard of the space race. Maybe you were intrigued by the words "hidden history" on the cover. Or maybe you've already learned about it in history textbooks and think it's "old news."

I thought I knew the story, too. But what the textbooks never told me was that the greatest, most visible race humankind has ever undertaken was won in the shadows by a former Nazi and a Russian who was jailed for crimes against his country. The story begins at the end of World War II with these two brilliant but controversial men. Wernher von Braun was a German Nazi officer, engineer, and eventual immigrant to the United States who came to America (under questionable circumstances, as you will see) to teach the US Army how to build rockets. Sergei Korolev was a celebrated Russian engineer in his own right, who was once imprisoned as a traitor to his country. By 1957, Korolev and von Braun were on opposite sides of the space race. This world-changing contest would bring stunning victories and tragic losses to both sides as Korolev and von Braun fought to be the first to reach the moon. They were strangers who never met, but their rivalry would alter the contours of science, politics, warfare, and space travel. However, despite their importance to one of the most astounding achievements in human history, crucial details of their lives and work were deliberately hidden from the public for decades.

So what does any of this have to do with you? The space race is over. The United States won when Apollo 11 landed on the moon in July 1969. Surely that's the end of the story, right? In a way, it's just the beginning, because von Braun's and Korolev's influence is all around us today. The rockets they perfected as spaceships were also intercontinental ballistic missiles (ICBMs)—weapons of mass destruction that can carry nuclear warheads thousands of miles and threaten every life on this planet, including yours.

The tensions at the heart of the space race between the United States and Russia (then known as the Soviet Union) reverberate in the twenty-first century. As I write this book, media headlines from around the world read like a spy thriller. Russia hacked America's presidential election in 2016 in an attempt to undermine democracy. The American president has been accused of colluding with the Russians to win that election illegally. All the while, 250 miles above Earth, aboard the International Space Station (ISS), American astronauts and Russian cosmonauts routinely cooperate in the name of science. Cooperation between the two countries expanded when the US ended its space shuttle program in 2011. For nine years, the US paid the Russians to carry American astronauts to the ISS aboard their Soyuz rocket, a vehicle originally developed under Sergei Korolev's leadership in the 1960s. America's triumphant return to crewed spaceflight from US soil came in May 2020, when the SpaceX Falcon 9 rocket and its Crew Dragon spacecraft launched NASA astronauts Douglas Hurley and Robert Behnken safely to the ISS.

Against this backdrop, the United States has set its sights on a return to the moon and a crewed landing on the surface of Mars by the 2030s. As humankind prepares to take the next "giant leap" deeper into the cosmos, now is the perfect moment to look back at the once-hidden history of the space race for clues about how to face the future. A new countdown is about to begin. This time, you'll be there to witness it. How will you record its history?

STAGE I

The Quest for Rockets

CHAPTER 1

THE OSENBERG LIST

When the Polish lab technician plunged his hand into the toilet bowl of a University of Bonn bathroom to retrieve a bundle of half-flushed papers, he couldn't have known he held a clue to one of Hitler's darkest secrets.

It was late March 1945. Adolf Hitler's reign of terror was finally drawing to a close, and British intelligence officers had received an important lead on Nazi activity in Bonn, Germany. Communication reports suggested that the University of Bonn's faculty could be burning evidence that linked them to war crimes. After the Allies overtook the university, the lab technician came forward with the mysterious papers. He told a British soldier that he had discovered them shoved into a toilet bowl, as if someone had tried to flush them. He had a hunch the documents might be important to the Allies. After all, why would someone try to flush ordinary documents down a toilet?

The lab technician was right to be suspicious. This "toilet paper" was part of a larger file that would come to be known as the Osenberg[1] List, a classified roster of Hitler's most notable—and notorious—scientists and engineers, some of whom had been building a lethal arsenal for the Nazis, like stockpiles of biological weapons capable of infecting and killing an entire population. Others were doctors who had conducted unspeakable experiments on concentration camp prisoners, and engineers who designed Hitler's high-tech mechanical weapons. If the Allies could locate these valuable military assets and interrogate their inventors, they could use the information to better protect their troops from Nazi attacks and learn their secrets as well. One engineer in particular was of great interest to the American army, and among the most wanted men in the world: Dr. Wernher von Braun. As the Nazis' genius rocket designer, he had invented the A-4 rocket, one of the deadliest weapons in Hitler's arsenal of *Wunderwaffen*, or "wonder weapons." The vehicle was renamed to match the terror it inspired. They called it the V-2.

The *V* stood for vengeance.

At almost four stories tall, this marvel of aeronautical engineering was the world's first ballistic missile. It was loaded with explosives and launched into a vertical arc, or trajectory, its powerful engine

---

1 The Osenberg List was compiled and maintained by Dr. Werner Osenberg, a mechanical engineer, a member of Hitler's SS, and a high-ranking member of the Gestapo, the Nazis' secret police.

thrusting the rocket to an altitude of fifty miles—the edge of outer space—making it the first man-made object to reach such an altitude. After its fuel reserves were exhausted, the rocket turned and plummeted back toward the Earth, propelled by gravity at more than five times the speed of sound, too fast to be detected or stopped.

A V-2 rocket launches from the Peenemünde Army Research Center, around 1937.

The Germans had used the V-2 missiles, each one capped with a one-ton warhead, to bombard Paris, London, and Antwerp, Belgium, since early September 1944. The constant threat of deadly V-2 attacks terrorized Western Europe. The British government ordered mass evacuations of its cities and issued millions of gas masks to civilians. People lived in a state of fear. But as deadly and destructive as the bombings were to populated cities, the V-2 had been deployed too late in the war to help Hitler defeat the Allies. Their persistent bombing campaigns from traditional aircraft were already overwhelming the Germans.

Von Braun's technology was years ahead of that of any other country in the world, and the American government had no intention of allowing it to be seized by the other Allied nations, especially the Soviet Union. The US-Soviet alliance against Hitler had been temporary as they fought to defeat their common enemy. The United States and the USSR knew that the deep philosophical differences between them would continue to divide the two countries after the war ended. The Soviet Union was a communist country intent on spreading its communist ideals to other nations. In contrast, the US wanted to contain communism at any cost in order to ensure the advancement of American capitalism around the world. This fundamental disagreement was positioned as freedom and democracy versus communism. But that was propaganda. In truth, it was communism versus capitalism.

Securing the V-2 for the US was crucial for another reason: military power. If the rocket could be paired with America's new nuclear weapon, the United States would become the greatest military force in the world. But where were the weapons manufactured? How many V-2s did Germany have?

And most important: Where was the V-2's inventor, Dr. Werner von Braun?

Von Braun, 1930s.

Subject: DR. WERNHER VON BRAUN

Status: Wanted by governments of the Allies as the mastermind of the Nazis' V-2 weapon.

Date and Place of Birth: March 23, 1912, Wirsitz, Germany

Occupation: Technical director of the Nazis' Peenemünde Army Research Center

Family: The middle child in an aristocratic German landholding family. Parents are Emmy von Braun and Magnus von Braun Sr. He has two siblings: Magnus von Braun Jr. and Sigismund von Braun.

Education: Earned a PhD in physics from the University of Berlin by the age of twenty-two. His dissertation on liquid-fuel rockets was considered so sensitive to national interests that the German army code-named and classified it.

Party Affiliation: Member of the National Socialist German Workers' Party (aka the Nazi Party) since 1937.

Other Affiliations: SS-Sturmbannführer (major) in the SS (Schutzstaffel, or Protection Squad): Originally established as Adolf Hitler's personal bodyguard unit, it would later become both the elite guard of the Nazi Reich and Hitler's executive force, prepared to "carry out all security-related duties, without regard for legal restraint."

Special Skills: Experienced pilot; avid horseman; sailor

Location: Unknown . . .

CHAPTER 2

THE HONORED NAZI

Three months earlier . . .

Northwestern Germany, near the village of Osterwick

From the outside, eight-hundred-year-old Castle Varlar looked like it belonged in a fairy tale. As the well-dressed guests arrived on the night of December 9, 1944, they admired its grand medieval architecture. The rolling, snow-covered grounds had once been home to a monastery, a holy place of worship. But inside the castle, the idyllic setting crumbled into a sinister reality. Red-black-and-white Nazi flags covered the walls. No detail had been spared, down to the eagle-and-swastika emblem on each china place setting around the lavish banquet table. The formal affair at the castle would be a night to remember, filled with food, drink, and, later, fireworks.[2]

The Nazis were celebrating. Four of Hitler's best technical

2   It's possible that the Knight's Cross award ceremony took place at a different castle, Schloss Berg.

minds, including his star rocket engineer, Dr. Wernher von Braun, were receiving the Knight's Cross of the War Service Cross, one of Hitler's highest noncombat honors. With wavy blond hair, blue eyes, and an athletic build, the thirty-two-year-old von Braun looked more like a movie star than an intellectual that night. He came from a wealthy German pedigree, embodying Hitler's twisted ideal of a white master race.

Also among the honorees was von Braun's boss and mentor, Walter Dornberger, an engineer and general in the German army. He invented a mobile launchpad for the V-2, a revolutionary contribution that made it possible to fire the weapon quickly and from almost any location. Dornberger had recruited von Braun at the age of nineteen to work for the German army. The skilled soldier and operative taught his brilliant but idealistic protégé how to navigate the complexities of working within the Nazi regime.

Wernher von Braun's trademark confidence and charm would have been on full display during the party. He reveled in the spotlight and lavished attention on others, making a person feel as if they were the only one in the room who mattered. When crossing paths with fellow SS officers, he would have raised his right hand in the Nazi salute and said, "Heil Hitler," in his distinctly nasal voice, a sound mismatched to his broad, six-foot frame.

The partygoers assembled and the ceremony began. After the first of the four medals was awarded, the hall was abruptly plunged into darkness. The diners watched as the drapes of a large nearby window were whisked open, as if to reveal a stage. Outside, a mobile launchpad with its V-2 rocket had been moved into full view of the captivated spectators. Its liquid fuel ignited, and "the room was suddenly lit with the flickering light of the rocket's exhaust," Walter Dornberger recalled. As the V-2 roared upward and disappeared into the sky, the reverberations from the missile's engine shook the old castle's walls. After each of the three remaining Knight's Cross medals was awarded, the scene was repeated, and another V-2 was launched in honor of the recipient.

The rockets that launched from Castle Varlar that night were more than elaborate special effects, however. They were weapons of mass destruction, targeting the city of Antwerp, Belgium, in order to weaken its port, a crucial asset of the Allies.

The City of Sudden Death

The V-2s launched from Castle Varlar would reach Antwerp in a matter of minutes. Just 137 miles away, eighteen-year-old Charles Ostyn worked in the city as a drafting apprentice. "It was like a streak from a comet," he said of witnessing the V-2 in flight. "As fast as a shooting star."

Fast and deadly. In contrast to Ostyn's poetic description of the V-2's flight, its impact was a sickening spectacle of crumbled buildings and wailing sirens. Emergency vehicles raced to the scene, and medical personnel scrambled to bandage the bleeding. The dead were hauled out of the rubble as scraps of clothing, metal, and glass debris rained down on the devastation. There had been no warning, no time for an alarm, because the rocket traveled faster than the speed of sound. In a cruel twist of the laws of physics, the whine of the V-2's approach was heard too late to serve as a warning; the sound arrived *after* the missile had already exploded.

V-2s also rained fire on London and Paris during the war. But because of its strategic importance to the Allies, Antwerp endured the worst of Hitler's V-2 attacks—and was hit with nearly two thousand vengeance weapons. Some 3,700 civilians were killed. Belgians nicknamed it the "City of Sudden Death," since the bombings happened frequently and without warning. Life in Antwerp left people like Ostyn terrified, without any hope that the relentless bombings would end.

Back at Castle Varlar, though, the awestruck party guests had no idea that von Braun was privately conspiring to betray Hitler. He and a handful of loyal coconspirators planned to abandon Germany and surrender to the United States. The decision had been made almost a year earlier, in January 1944, when von Braun convened a secret meeting of his most trusted associates to discuss the future of the V-2 rocket. Two things had become clear to them. First, Germany was going to lose the war. Hitler had initially doubted the V-2's capacity to turn the tide in his favor and delayed its deployment. By the time he was convinced of the rocket's potential, his empire known as the Third Reich was in tatters, barely holding its own against the Allies.

Second, the group agreed that no matter what happened in the final months of the war, von Braun's visionary rocket development work must not be destroyed when Germany fell. They were secret partners in a dream to use the V-2 for something more inspiring than warfare. Because of its ability to climb to the edge of outer space, the V-2 was the world's first glimpse of interplanetary travel. This weapon of mass destruction also had the potential to be a humanitarian tool of scientific discovery. It was a bold and ambitious dream with world-changing possibilities—and life-and-death stakes. If anyone found out what they were plotting, the conspirators could be accused of treason, arrested, and executed.

By studying applications of the V-2 technology for interplanetary travel, they were disobeying Hitler's decree that every German, including women and children, devote everything—even their lives—to defeating the Allies. Von Braun was well aware of the precarious nature of his group's position. If they were caught, they risked the wrath of Heinrich Himmler, the fanatical head of Hitler's elite SS guard. Himmler was the key senior Nazi official responsible for the planning and implementation of the "Final Solution," the Nazi genocide of the Jews of Europe, and he had already jailed von Braun once before.

The story goes that von Braun drank too much alcohol at a party and someone overheard him talking about using the V-2 as a spaceship. His drunken, treasonous remarks eventually reached Himmler, who had the rocket engineer arrested by the SS. Von Braun wasn't just any prisoner, and Himmler knew it. He was protected by his privileged position within the Nazi establishment as the V-2 inventor—prestige that ensured that von Braun was not harmed while in custody. It didn't hurt that von Braun also had friends in very high places, who were leveraging their influence on his behalf. After just two weeks of relatively comfortable confinement, his mentor, Walter Dornberger, and Albert Speer, Hitler's minister of armaments and war production, succeeded. Von Braun was released, but he knew that privilege and powerful contacts wouldn't save him a second time if Himmler found out he and his associates were planning to betray the Nazis. The group's only hope for a future in rocketry was to escape Germany and surrender to the Americans. Von Braun believed the United States had enough money to support and sustain a space exploration program. He was risking his team's lives and his own in trusting that America would make his dream come true.

CHAPTER 3

RISE OF THE ROCKET FANATIC

Since childhood, von Braun had dreamed of building a rocket to reach outer space. His obsession ignited on March 23, 1925, when his mother, an intellectual with an interest in science, gave him a small telescope for his thirteenth birthday. His observations of the moon and stars captivated the youngster. But viewing the heavens through a telescope would never be enough. Von Braun wanted to build a rocket, climb aboard, and use it to travel to the moon.

Blessed with an agile mind and insatiable curiosity, von Braun enjoyed the study of foreign languages and the arts. He excelled as a musician, playing both the piano and cello. For a time, he considered becoming a composer. In school, von Braun preferred the role of class clown to teacher's pet, and his grades, especially those in mathematics, suffered. He simply refused to focus on subjects that did not interest him. He preferred reading the imaginative science-fiction tales of Jules Verne and H. G. Wells. Homework was a bore. He wanted to work with his hands. Inspired by Henry Ford, the American automobile inventor, von Braun's favorite pastime was rebuilding an old car in the family garage.

At age sixteen, he powered a wooden children's wagon with a crude engine made entirely of fireworks. When it took off, the contraption streaked down the family's Berlin street. "It swerved this way and that, zigzagging through groups," von Braun recalled years later. "I yelled a warning and men and women fled in all directions. I was ecstatic. The wagon was wholly out of control and trailing a comet's tail of fire."

The police arrived and von Braun's displeased father grounded him for a day, but his mother confessed that it was impossible to stay angry with him for long. "Whenever I tried, he would put on his most cherubic smile and talk about something else," she said. "He had no problem learning good manners, and he usually practiced them. When he did not, it was just a brief spell of naughtiness, or simply his own way of expressing an exuberant joy of life." Von Braun was less exuberant in his schoolwork, and his grades reflected the lack of effort. The school notified his parents that their son would have to repeat the eighth grade. The von Brauns refused to hold him back. Instead, he was transferred to a boarding school to complete grades eight through ten. It was here, during his first term, that his interest in space travel took off.

Putting him into Ettersburg School, 124 miles southwest of Berlin, the von Brauns hoped their son would finally transform into an accomplished student, but despite their worried pleas, von Braun would not apply himself to schoolwork. One afternoon in his room, he picked up a magazine. As he flipped through its pages, an advertisement for a book caught his eye: *Die Rakete zu den Planetenräumen* (*The Rocket into Interplanetary Space*) by Hermann Oberth. Rockets! Now there was a subject he could get excited about. He ordered a copy.

When it finally arrived in his school mailbox, von Braun raced to his room, eager to explore Oberth's theories. But when he opened the book, it was undecipherable. "I was appalled by the fact that it was filled with mathematical equations," he said years later. To his dismay, Oberth had written his book in two of the languages von Braun had failed to learn: mathematics and physics. Terrified of never being able to comprehend the book and desperate for help, von Braun rushed to his teachers. "What can I do to understand this book?" he demanded. They told him that in order to understand Oberth's work, he would have to master his two worst subjects. It was a defining moment in his life. Almost overnight, von Braun became a model student. His grades in math and science improved dramatically. Soon after, he began writing a physics textbook and sketched illustrations of a future spaceship.

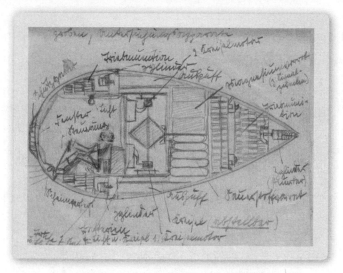

Von Braun's illustration of his future spaceship.

After finishing tenth grade at Ettersburg, von Braun enrolled in the Lietz School in northwestern Germany to complete his secondary schooling and prepare for college. It stood on the remote island of Spiekeroog, in the North Sea. While his friends attended parties and dated, von Braun's studies intensified. His newly directed intellect and drive to succeed were a relief to his parents and an asset to his teachers and fellow students. He worked as a tutor, helping classmates with their schoolwork. When an instructor fell ill, he stepped in as a faculty substitute—despite the fact that the course was above his grade level. "By day I taught. By night I tutored," he said. "Between times I studied my own lessons."

By the time von Braun graduated in April 1930—a full year ahead of schedule—he had outgrown his reputation as a class clown and emerged as a disciplined academic who knew his life's purpose. Wernher von Braun had evolved into a full-blown rocket fanatic.

Von Braun, (second row far right) as an eighteen-year-old rocket enthusiast attending a launch in July 1930.

He was not alone in his enthusiasm for technology. Europe in the 1930s was gripped by a rocket craze. Science-fiction films like *Metropolis* and *Woman in the Moon* by the famous director Fritz Lang inspired amateur rocketeers to invent their own fantastic vehicles. Von Braun watched as real-life daredevils in leather jackets, helmets, and goggles climbed aboard fast and dangerous rocket-powered cars, racing around tracks and roaring down city streets.

These amateur rocket designers dreamed of their inventions

reaching outer space, but defying the laws of nature was expensive, and their only capital was creativity. To succeed, they needed money to pay for parts and fuel. For most people in 1932, rocket building probably looked like an exciting but weird hobby that could blow up in your face. For von Braun, who was now studying mechanical engineering at the Charlottenburg Institute of Technology, the rocket enthusiasts were a like-minded community of people who shared his obsession. He joined forces with a group of headstrong rocket builders headquartered in an abandoned munitions dump in Berlin, known as the Raketenflugplatz (Rocketport). Von Braun became a prominent member of the group and was instrumental in the successful launch of their first homemade liquid-fueled rocket. Powerful people began to take notice.

Since the end of World War I in 1918, the Germans had been desperate to rebuild their military. The conflict began when Germany invaded Belgium on August 4, 1914. Belgium's ally, Great Britain, responded by declaring war on Germany, sparking a bloody four-year war involving ten countries, which ravaged Europe, killing an estimated forty million people.

ROCKET CRAZE

Today it's difficult to imagine a time without rockets, but in the 1930s, they were still highly experimental. World governments had not yet discovered how to effectively apply rocket technology to warfare, let alone use rockets to travel into space.

The Treaty of Versailles ended the war and outlined the penalties Germany had to pay for starting the conflict. Among other restrictions, the treaty forbade the German military from rebuilding its weapons arsenal by manufacturing tanks, submarines, airplanes, and other armaments. The treaty, however, held no provision against rocket development. The technology was still in its infancy, but if this new invention could be produced affordably and deployed as a weapon, Germany would gain a secret military advantage. Among the amateur rocketeers, few were as eager to prove themselves as the ambitious Wernher von Braun.

An Irresistible Offer

It was a spring day in 1932 when German Army captain Walter Dornberger arrived in a black car in front of the Raketenflugplatz headquarters. The German army had been keeping tabs on the young band of rocket fanatics, and von Braun stood out from the others. Dornberger recalled being impressed with his energetic work ethic and "astonishing theoretical knowledge." The army offered to fund the group's experimental rocket work. The only condition was that their experiments be carried out under the utmost secrecy on the secure grounds of an army post.

Twenty-year-old von Braun was elated. It was a generous offer, and experimenting with rockets for the army in exchange for funding seemed reasonable. The potential military applications of the technology were not entirely unknown to him at the time. His hero,

Hermann Oberth, had suggested as much in his writings, but it remained only a theoretical possibility. The German army wanted von Braun to develop rockets for defense, but von Braun would later say that he hadn't cared what the army's motives were. He and his fellow Raketenflugplatz members needed money, and the army was willing to give it to them. In 1932, the Nazis had not yet come to power. It was peacetime. Von Braun wasn't worried about the possible future applications of his rockets as weapons. He was obsessed with space exploration. "To me, the Army's money was the only hope for big progress toward space travel," he later said. The possibility that one of his inventions could be deployed as a weapon, or what it could one day destroy, did not figure into the calculus of his moral code. The rocket itself was all that mattered to him.

Within four years, von Braun's relationship with the German army had expanded beyond his wildest dreams. The Germans had such confidence in his abilities and the future applications of his technology that they planned to build a top secret, state-of-the-art rocket manufacturing facility. The Peenemünde Army Research Center would be the first of its kind in the world. If von Braun— then only twenty-four years old—had any doubts about his growing importance to the German military, they were soon dispelled by his new role as the research center's technical director.

The construction site was the tiny fishing village of Peenemünde (pronounced pay-neh-*moon*-duh), located in a remote section of northern Germany on the Baltic Sea. Von Braun's mother, Emmy, suggested the site, reminding her son of the area's natural isolation and how much their family had loved visiting there to vacation and hunt. Peenemünde, with its tall pine trees, marshes, and abundant wildlife, was largely undeveloped, with fewer than five hundred residents. Its only structures were ninety-six houses and a single school.

To clear the path for construction of the highly classified facility, local residents were forced from their land but were at least paid fairly for it. Before long, the tiny seaside village had vanished and Peenemünde's technological transformation was underway.

By May 1937, the first manufacturing plants had been completed and rocket tests began. Von Braun proved himself a hands-on leader with a remarkable talent for keeping track of the growing manufacturing enterprise and its workers. The people who worked for von Braun held their leader in the highest regard because he rarely lost his cool when things went wrong. Once, an engineer confessed to a mistake that caused a rocket to fly off course, and von Braun rewarded his honesty with a bottle of champagne. He wanted his team to trust him, especially when they fell short of his expectations, because it was the only way to ensure the error wasn't repeated on future tests.

While von Braun was honing his people skills and building a career with the German army, Adolf Hitler came to power. In November 1937, von Braun was invited to join the Nazi Party, and he accepted. His pivotal role in the German national defense and his dependence on powerful political connections within the Nazi Party made it difficult for him to refuse. The degree to which he may have been coerced is unclear, but a statement he made years later sheds light on his decision. "My refusal to join the party would have meant that I would have to abandon the work of my life. Therefore I decided to join. My membership did not involve any political activity." Von Braun may have claimed little interest in the details of day-to-day politics, but his rocket work was inseparable from the evil actions of the Nazi regime that paid his salary and funded his research.

On September 1, 1939, Hitler invaded Poland, and World War II erupted. As the war raged for six years, the Nazis murdered six million Jews for failing to meet Hitler's cruel criteria for creating a perfect master race. Others, too, were targeted by the regime, including anti-Hitler German politicians and resistance activists, Soviet civilians and prisoners of war, non-Jewish Polish civilians, Serbs, Roma, and homosexuals. The physically disabled and mentally ill were also executed. All told, as many as sixty million soldiers and civilians perished in the conflict. These crimes and casualties are among the worst and most well-known facts defining World War II in history books. However, these often-repeated statistics are so overwhelming in scale that they helped conceal a lesser-known story buried deep inside a mountain cave in central Germany, near the small town of Nordhausen. It was here that von Braun's connection to Hitler's crimes was hidden.

CHAPTER 4

CAMP DORA

April 11, 1945

Central Germany

By the spring of 1945, Army private John Galione felt grateful to have survived the war thus far, but it was the mission, not good fortune, that was now driving Galione and the soldiers of the US Army's 104th Army Infantry Division, known as the Timberwolves. The soldiers were to assist in the liberation of the Mittelbau-Dora concentration camp (also known as Camp Dora) outside the city of Nordhausen in central Germany. But nothing the battle-weary Galione had witnessed in the war prepared him and his fellow soldiers for what they found that early spring day.

The corpses of approximately five thousand starved prisoners were strewn across the sprawling grounds and inside the camp's buildings. Some of the victims had died in a recent bombing raid by the Allies. But evidence of the Nazis' murderous cruelty was everywhere. The army medics choked back tears as they found more bodies "stacked like cordwood" beneath a staircase in one of the barracks.

This memorial sculpture by artist Jürgen von Woyski stands in front of the cremantorium at Camp Mittelbau-Dora.

"The people were so happy to see us," Galione remembered. "They were tugging our clothes, thanking us, hugging us . . . feeling our uniforms between their fingers like they were gold. They just wanted to touch us; thanking God over and over again . . . they looked like the walking dead. They were skin and bones . . . some of them were so weak they didn't even live long enough to be rescued."

It is estimated that sixty thousand people had passed through the

Camp Dora system during the war. Members of the Timberwolves were haunted by what they had seen, and some were so traumatized, they refused to speak of it for the rest of their lives.

Adjacent to Camp Dora was the entrance to an old gypsum mine hidden inside Kohnstein Mountain. After the Allies bombed the Peenemünde Army Research Center in August 1943 and severely damaged the facility, the Nazis relocated the factory to the abandoned mine. Mittelwerk—German for "central works"—became the new manufacturing center of the V-2. Buried inside the mountain's network of tunnels, the V-2 operation would be hidden from Allied planes. Before manufacturing could begin, however, the mine required additional improvements to expand it into a rocket production facility.

That job fell to another barbaric SS officer, Brigadier General Hans Kammler. The civil engineer and ardent Nazi supervised the upgrades at Mittelwerk. The general's sadistic claim to fame was the prominent role he played in building the ultrasecret extermination camps and gas chambers at Auschwitz-Birkenau, Majdanek, and Belzec. At Auschwitz-Birkenau alone, between two of its chambers, approximately four thousand people could be murdered at one time.

At Mittelwerk, Kammler used concentration camp forced labor to blast deeper into Kohnstein Mountain and expand the railroad tunnels that would transport equipment and parts into the facility and carry finished rockets out of it. The inmates came from all over

Europe, but mostly from the Soviet Union, Poland, and France, and had been arrested for political reasons. Beginning in May 1944, Jews were also deported to the camp. They cleared debris after dynamite blasts and loaded the heavy rocks into railcars by hand.

The conditions under which prisoners were forced to live and work inside the tunnels were abominable. Before crude barracks were constructed at Camp Dora, thousands slept in rancid, lice-infested bunks, not seeing daylight for months. There was no heat or running water. Even in the summer their bodies were cold. The temperature inside the dank mountain tunnel was a near-constant forty-two degrees. Compounding the misery was the absence of adequate bathroom facilities. Large barrels served as toilets—and there weren't enough of those. Dysentery and typhus were rampant. Weakened by disease and hunger, some prisoners fell to their deaths from thirty-foot scaffolds as they churned out the V-2 rockets in backbreaking twelve-hour shifts. Some dropped dead where they stood. Others were crushed beneath heavy machinery or falling rubble after explosions.

Survivor Albert van Dijk remembered his first day of incarceration inside the tunnels, which reeked of human waste, death, metal, and dust. Van Dijk had watched as a group of malnourished prisoners strained under the heavy loads they were forced to carry. "They were crawling on their knees and carrying heavy rocks . . . there were corpses on the floor. It was terrible." Van Dijk's job was to tally the dead. "Sometimes I was so depressed that I lay down on the floor, or looked for a dark corner and wanted to die. I didn't even know my own name anymore."

It was a miracle van Dijk survived. A strong and healthy man could expect to live six months in Mittelwerk before dying of starvation, if he managed to keep up the inhuman pace of work for that long. Estimates put the death toll average at 160 people per day. Victims died from severe mistreatment; some were murdered in cold blood. Ruthless guards shot many prisoners outright, while others were executed in mass hangings as their fellow prisoners were forced to watch. When work resumed, they had to walk past the dangling bodies, a dire warning against resistance, laziness, or plots of sabotage. An estimated twenty thousand of these forced laborers died in the manufacturing of the V-2 rockets at Mittelwerk—more than were killed by the rocket itself during the war. Amid this unimaginable human suffering, the V-2 weapon rolled off the assembly line.

Wernher von Braun witnessed the horrible conditions inside Mittelwerk. He visited the facility as many as fifteen times and handpicked prisoners with education and engineering skill for specialized projects. Von Braun's job as head of Nazi rocket development automatically made him a part of the Mittelwerk system. He was not in control of the entire V-2 operation at the plant—his Nazi superiors were—and they required him to analyze the rocket production schedule to maximize its productivity. To that end, he calculated the most efficient ratio between skilled German workers and forced laborers. Regarding those calculations, he wrote a memo:

*In view of the difficulty of the testing processes to be
carried out there, the ratio of prisoners to German skilled
workers for the foreseeable future cannot exceed 2:1.*

This series of handwritten calculations is physical evidence of his knowledge of forced labor. And his participation in a decision to use it in the manufacturing of his rockets suggests he may indeed have been guilty of a crime against humanity—a war crime—punishable by death.

However, von Braun was never tried and convicted of a war crime, and therefore the question of his guilt or innocence remains officially undetermined. While no proof has ever surfaced to support that von Braun was prejudiced against Jews, or made anti-Semitic statements, neither is there evidence to suggest that he was concerned about what was happening to them during the war. Nor does he appear to have been a devoted Nazi fanatic like Himmler or Kammler, however. Von Braun did not wear the black dress uniform and armband unless it was required, and omitted his rank from official correspondence The reason why von Braun may have rejected consistent use of these symbols of his SS membership is unknown, but it's possible that his choices reflected the rocket designer's general disinterest in party politics. One engineer reported that when he once expressed surprise at seeing von Braun in the uniform, the rocket designer replied, "There was no way around it."

But these facts hardly qualify as active resistance against Hitler's policies and fail to absolve him of moral responsibility. Von Braun chose not to speak out against the lethal conditions inside the V-2 factory or halt his work in protest. What if he had? Would someone else have been able to carry on in his place, or would he have been arrested—or executed? We'll never know.

Indeed, if von Braun was fanatically devoted to anything, it was his lifelong goal of building a rocket to the moon, and nothing—not the deaths of thousands of concentration camp prisoners, or even Adolf Hitler himself—would stand in his way.

CHAPTER 5

BETRAYING HITLER

By April 30, 1945, Adolf Hitler had more pressing concerns than the whereabouts of Wernher von Braun. Two and a half million Red Army troops swarmed Berlin with six thousand Russian tanks and more than forty thousand artillery weapons to crush what was left of the Nazi regime. The war Hitler had started was almost over, and it was not ending at all like the dictator had imagined. The bloody Battle of Berlin had raged for two weeks between the Nazis and the Soviets, killing hundreds of thousands of soldiers and countless civilian men, women, and children. Facing defeat and certain death, Hitler hid underground in a secret bunker fifty feet beneath Germany's capital. While his people fought and died in his name, he had sequestered himself there for five months with his partner, Eva Braun. When confronted with the choice to fight for his life, he did not go down battling to his last breath the way he had demanded of all German citizens. Rather than risk arrest or death at the hands of the Russians, Hitler and Braun committed suicide.

The next day, Germans learned of Hitler's death in a somber radio announcement that failed to disclose that he had taken his own life. With the loss of Hitler, the war in Europe was ending, but Hitler's fanatical followers were determined to carry out his last wishes. The previous month, Hitler had issued a "scorched earth" policy. If the Allies won, the Third Reich and Germany would burn in a fire they would set themselves, leaving nothing for the Allies but ashes.

In the aftermath of Hitler's death, von Braun and his associates realized their moment had come. They had to surrender before Himmler could have them shot or use them as leverage against the Allies to save himself. Either way, everything von Braun had worked for—and his dream of space travel—was at risk with every minute that passed. He doubted the Soviets' Red Army would welcome the Nazis' lead rocket designer with open arms. Would they execute him on sight? Arrest him? There was another possibility, of course. They could offer to fund his research if he agreed to build rockets for the Soviet Union. But he knew the Russians didn't have the financial resources to fund the rocket program he wanted. America did. The country's wealth would be crucial if he had any hope of reaching outer space with his rockets. It was a dangerous gamble, but von Braun liked his odds. Would he be greeted as a valuable scientific asset or an enemy of the United States government? There was only one way to find out.

Two days later, on May 2, 1945, von Braun's twenty-five-year-old brother, Magnus, set off to initiate the group's surrender. "I hopped on my bike with nothing else but a story," he later wrote, and set off down a steep, foggy mountain road known as Adolf Hitler Pass. It was spring, but stubborn snow clung to the ground. Patches of green pasture were visible here and there. The season's first flowers strained toward light and warmth, but there was not yet enough of either to melt the brittle, frozen earth. Behind Magnus, Wernher and a group of his trusted engineers were sequestered at a ski lodge, Haus Ingeborg, near the Austrian border. Magnus served as messenger because he spoke the best English. The plan was simple but bold. He would ride directly into the path of the nearby American troops, betting his life that they would hear him out before they fired a shot.

When US Army private Fred Schneikert of Sheboygan, Wisconsin, looked up from his post, he saw a young man pedaling a bicycle in the distance, just beyond where he and the 44th Infantry Division anti-tank platoon were stationed. The cautious private held his ground and raised his rifle as the man eased his bicycle to a stop and began to speak in German-accented English. He identified himself as Magnus von Braun. He told Schneikert that his brother was Wernher von Braun, the designer of the V-2 rocket.

Scheinkert immediately summoned intelligence officers, who must have been eager to verify that one of the most wanted Nazi engineering teams had just fallen into their laps. "They showed up with a carton of Camels," Magnus von Braun recalled. Cigarettes were rare treats when such luxuries were rationed, if they were available at all. By late afternoon, von Braun's plan had worked just as he'd hoped. He and his team had escaped the German and Soviet armies and were safe in the custody of the United States government.

Von Braun and his brother Magnus on the day of their surrender to the US Army. Von Braun, in a cast, had broken his arm in a car accident in the days leading up to their surrender.

Now the only remaining problem was how American intelligence officers were going to get the Nazi scientists into the United States.

The solution was a classified military project called Operation Paperclip. What sounded like a clandestine trip to an office supply store was actually the code name for a top secret plan to relocate one thousand German scientists, engineers, and other technicians into the United States. Given the sensitive nature of their expertise, and the fact that some of the Paperclip participants had been Nazis, it was easier to cover up their past than explain it to the American public. The project was named for the discreet procedure used to mark the dossiers of those included in the program. A paper clip was attached to each file, signaling which Germans would bypass the legal US immigration system. Intelligence officials were in a hurry to learn from these experts, especially von Braun and approximately 350 members of his team, whose V-2 technology could revolutionize American military defenses.

At its inception, Operation Paperclip was a temporary program to acquire German scientific intelligence that could benefit the United States. Each person selected would receive a six-month contract to work in the US. Nazi Party members, officers in Hitler's SS, or recipients of Nazi awards were to be disqualified. Some of the Paperclip participants fit into one or more of these disqualifying categories, but they were considered so valuable by the US military that they were allowed to secretly enter the country anyway. Such was the case with von Braun, who met all three criteria. Membership in the Nazi Party was not uncommon at the time. Hitler's authoritarian government consisted of a single party, the Nazis. Von Braun had been pressured to join because of his importance to rocketry and national defense. His status as an officer in the SS who had received numerous Nazi awards was more problematic. These two most damaging facts about his past became part of von Braun's highly classified record within the secret army program, concealing what were believed to be his worst offenses.

Von Braun, however, knew the truth. He had darker secrets than a rank in Hitler's SS and Nazi honors pinned to his uniform. He had witnessed the deadly conditions inside Mittelwerk. What would he say if confronted by American intelligence with questions about his connection to the underground rocket factory and its adjacent concentration camp? If he told the truth, would he be allowed to enter the US as part of Operation Paperclip or be detained as a criminal pending a war crimes investigation? Once again, luck was on von Braun's side. It seems impossible to fathom in hindsight, but no one appears to have asked the V-2 designer if he'd had any direct involvement in the underground V-2 factory. This fact is further complicated when you consider that the liberation of Camp Dora was common knowledge within the US military in Germany at the time, as were the atrocities at Mittelwerk, yet no one seems to have pressed von Braun for answers. Were intelligence officials simply careless in their mad dash to acquire von Braun and his technology for the US? Or is it probable that they didn't ask because they did not want to hear the truth? It is impossible to know for certain. However, the fact that the US Army was eager to use von Braun and his team to learn about their rocket technology and wanted to expedite their entry into the United States is well documented. Meanwhile, the German rocketeers maintained they were simply doing their jobs as ordered, and blamed Hitler's SS for everything else. By all accounts, it appears these excuses were enough to satisfy their interrogators.

With that, von Braun's most dangerous secret was hidden from his earliest interactions with the Americans. Like an unexploded land mine, it would remain buried for forty years.[3]

By late afternoon on September 18, 1945, any worries von Braun had about his hidden history would have been eclipsed by his hopes for the future. He and six members of his scientific team secretly departed for America. Everything was going just as he had planned. He had a six-month contract to teach the Americans how to fly his V-2 and was leaving his secret behind him, in the ruins of Hitler's Germany.[4]

While the events of Wernher von Braun's life to this point are extraordinary, they are only half the story. In the Soviet Union,

---

3 A rare photograph, which appears in *Von Braun: Dreamer of Space, Engineer of War*, by Michael J. Neufeld, shows a half-hidden Wernher von Braun wearing his black Nazi uniform walking with Heinrich Himmler and Walter Dornberger. Neufeld asserts in the image's caption that "it is almost certainly von Braun."

4 Walter Dornberger was detained in Germany for further questioning by the British and did not depart with von Braun on September 18, 1945. He eventually immigrated to the United States in 1947, after being cleared of war crimes by the British, and worked as an adviser to the US government on military missile technology.

another man was rising to claim his place in spaceflight history. Sergei Pavlovich Korolev was a brilliant engineer who was equally obsessed with rockets. But Korolev's quest for the moon would follow a different path than his privileged German rival's. Where did his story begin and how did he become one of the two most important people in the race to space? To find out, we must rewind the clock to June 27, 1938, two months before Hitler would invade Poland and begin World War II—and the worst day of Sergei Korolev's life.

Korolev's arrest photo.

Subject: SERGEI PAVLOVICH KOROLEV

Status: Suspected traitor. Classified as an enemy of the Russian people.

Date of and Place of Birth: January 12, 1907, Zhitomir, Ukraine

Occupation: Engineer, Reactive Scientific-Research Institute, Moscow, where he was employed as the deputy chief of the institute, developing missiles

Family: Ksenia Korolev (wife), Natalia Korolev (daughter)

Education: Bauman High Technical School, Moscow

Special Skills: Experienced pilot

Location: Moscow

CHAPTER 6

AN INNOCENT TRAITOR

A dark new moon rose over Moscow as thirty-one-year-old Sergei Korolev walked home from work to the apartment he shared with his wife, Ksenia, a medical student. The dark-eyed, barrel-chested Russian was an engineer at a top secret rocket research facility, the Reactive Scientific-Research Institute (RNII) in Moscow.

At RNII, he developed missiles for the Soviet government. It was thrilling to work with new technology, but it was a dangerous time for every Soviet citizen. Some of his colleagues at the institute were disappearing, and Korolev feared he would be next.

Josef Stalin, the country's paranoid communist dictator, was determined to eliminate political rivals at any cost. At that time, the Soviet Union, like Hitler's Germany, was an authoritarian state. In an authoritarian society, extreme secrecy dominates every aspect of life, isolating its people from the outside world and concealing crimes committed by their ruler. Stalin, like Hitler, was in complete control. People were encouraged to spy on one another and report any anti-Soviet activity. Since 1936, Stalin's brutal secret police force, the People's Commissariat for Internal Affairs (NKVD), had begun arresting Soviet citizens (many of them innocent of crimes) on false or fabricated charges.

It was a period of rampant arrests known as the Great Terror, during which Stalin sought to eliminate his enemies by incarcerating millions of innocent Soviet citizens. Without a trial or proof of guilt, anyone could be detained. There were whispers of people being abducted on the street and never heard from again. Most were wrongfully imprisoned in an elaborate system of labor camps known as the Gulag. Between 1929 and 1953 this network of barbed-wire labor camps and guard towers spanned the length and width of the Soviet Union and detained approximately eighteen million people.

Stalin's plan was twofold: he would remove his political enemies while simultaneously creating a prison labor force. Anyone he believed threatened his leadership or contradicted his authority was jailed. The prisoners farmed the land and mined the Soviet Union's rich mineral reserves. Stalin needed the gold trapped beneath the frozen Siberian tundra to trade with the West for technology and equipment to modernize his country.

No one was safe, not even the Soviet Union's greatest scientific minds. Korolev was already a suspect. One of his colleagues at the institute, a brilliant rocket engine designer named Valentin Glushko, had been accused of consorting with "enemies of the people" and deemed untrustworthy with military secrets. In March, the NKVD had arrested him. While other coworkers denounced Glushko in order to escape arrest, Korolev refused to lie and defended his colleague. A brave and selfless act that made him a target as well.

Hurrying along that summer evening, Korolev paused to buy a copy of *Pravda*, the official Soviet newspaper, and to pick up a loaf of French bread for supper. The couple would dine alone that night, as their only child, three-year-old Natalia, was visiting her grandmother. Later, it would prove fortunate that she had not been home.

Korolev climbed the stairs to the sixth floor and opened the door of their one-room apartment. Ksenia was still at work. Some time later, she arrived, nervous and afraid. There were men downstairs, she said. They were dressed in dark suits, asking questions and interviewing their neighbors. They looked like NKVD officers.

The arrival of the infamous black NKVD vehicles, known as "Black Ravens," filled everyone with dread. Some of the building's tenants had already been arrested. There was no way to be certain who they had come for this time, but Stalin's enforcers never left empty-handed. After supper, Sergei and Ksenia listened to music on their phonograph. They waited.

The doorbell rang.

Korolev opened the door and saw two NKVD officers, each carrying a semiautomatic Tokarev pistol. One of the men flashed official-looking credentials. They stepped inside and ordered Korolev to sit down.

When the NKVD entered the home of a suspected traitor, they tore through drawers, tossed furniture, and smashed anything that got in their way. Sentimental heirlooms crashed to the floor as they searched for papers, diaries, and scraps of circumstantial evidence that might incriminate the accused. The police found nothing suspicious in the Korolevs' apartment, but they arrested Sergei anyway.

He did not resist as he pulled on his old leather coat. Ksenia was desperate. She couldn't imagine where these men were taking her husband or how long he would be gone. "I naively gave him two changes of underwear for the journey," she remembered years later. "We said goodbye and kissed each other."

At the window she waited for one last glimpse of Sergei as the police led him to their car. She had no idea it was the last time she would see her husband for six years. "I had golden hair," she later said. "It went completely gray overnight."

While he was under arrest, interrogators broke Korolev's upper and lower jaws. After many beatings and episodes of torture, Korolev couldn't take any more. He falsely confessed to crimes of treason to end his suffering and appeared before a judge. After a fifteen-minute deliberation, he was found guilty and sentenced to ten years' hard labor. Korolev had escaped execution, but a quick death might have been a more humane punishment than his sentence. He would be imprisoned at Kolyma, the most feared and notorious Gulag camp, in extreme northeastern Siberia, only 217 miles south of the Arctic Circle.

Boy from a Broken Home

Sergei Korolev had been loyal to his country his entire life. He was born on January 12, 1907, in the Ukrainian town of Zhitomir, to a pair of academics. His father, Pavel, was a teacher at a girls' school, and his mother, Maria, taught French. A year after their son's birth, his parents separated and Korolev went to live with his grandparents. His new home was isolating but comfortable. There weren't many children to play with, and the young boy depended on his mother's aging parents for entertainment. At the age of six, he attended his first air show. From the safety of his grandfather's shoulders, he watched as the pilot climbed into the plane. To the little boy's amazment, it lifted off the ground and flew into the air. From that moment, young Sergei was mesmerized by flight.

As he matured, Korolev's passion for planes and flight intensified. When he was a teenager, he joined a local organization dedicated to the pursuit of flight, the Society of Friends of the Air Fleet. At seventeen, he designed his first glider. His family was skeptical of Korolev's fascination with aeronautics, worrying it was too dangerous and believing that it would be best for him to learn a trade. Out of respect for their wishes, the following year he found work with a construction crew as a roofer's apprentice.

But Korolev never lost his passion for flight. By 1930, he had graduated from the most elite engineering school in the Soviet Union, Bauman High Technical School, Moscow (an institution comparable to the Massachusetts Institute of Technology in the United States) and obtained his pilot's license. "Going up in the air," he said, "my thoughts turned more and more frequently to the creation of a jet engine." He daydreamed about ways to reach higher altitudes and greater distances. He continued to design gliders, but new possibilities were irresistible. Like von Braun, he sought a community of people who shared his passion, with whom he could design, build, and test liquid-fueled rockets.

Korolev seated inside one of the gliders he loved to build and fly.

After college, Korolev cofounded his own group of rocket enthusiasts called GIRD (Gruppa Isutcheniya Reaktivnovo Dvisheniya, or Group for the Investigation of Reactive Motion). Just as the German military discovered the potential of von Braun's early rocket experiments at the Raketenflugplatz, the Soviet government recognized the potential of Korolev and his fellow experimenters. Two years after its formation, GIRD was acquired by the Soviet military and renamed RNII (Reactive Scientific-Research Institute), the official center for research and the development of missiles. Korolev was appointed its deputy chief. Four years later, Joseph Stalin's "Great Terror" began and Korolev's life had unraveled.

In July 1939, Korolev arrived at the Siberian labor camp with five thousand other prisoners. Nothing distinguished him from the rest of the miserable masses fighting for survival. During his first few months, he suffered brutal beatings from guards or other prisoners, leaving a large scar on his head. Food was always in short supply. The malnourished prisoners subsisted on soup made of spoiled cabbage, potatoes, and the heads and lungs of fish. Korolev developed scurvy as a result of his vitamin-deficient diet, a condition that cost him fourteen teeth.

Diseases like typhus were a constant threat in the cramped, unsanitary quarters. Bedbugs and other parasites, such as lice, amplified the prisoners' suffering.

They were issued clothing or uniforms that fit poorly. Pants, shirts, and coats could be torn or threadbare. Other inmates didn't have shoes. After the short, sweltering, and mosquito-infested summer turned to winter, none of the garments were sufficient to insulate workers against the bone-chilling Siberian cold. At Camp Kolyma, some of the lowest temperatures on Earth were recorded. If the prisoners didn't die of exposure, they were worked to death, murdered by fellow inmates and guards, or perished from starvation or disease.

The winter after Korolev's arrival was one of the worst on record. Temperatures plunged to minus fifty degrees Fahrenheit. In this unforgiving environment, Korolev worked twelve hours a day digging gold for Joseph Stalin. He endured the misery of Kolyma for at least fifteen months.

Against overwhelming odds, he survived. He was then transferred several times over the next four and a half years between other types of Gulag camps. During these years, he drafted letters, pleading his case to anyone who would listen. "I am convicted of a crime I've never committed," he wrote to the chief prosecutor of the Soviet Union. "I have never been a member of any anti-Soviet organization." His indignation and anger dissolved into hopelessness in a letter to Ksenia. "I am so very tired of life," he wrote. "I can see no end to my dreadful situation."

In July 1944, Korolev and thirty-five other prisoners were abruptly released from specialized prisons, known as *sharashki*; workshops and laboratories where prisoners with technical or scientific expertise worked on government projects. Conditions in sharashki were a vast improvement over the Siberian labor camps. At the time of his release, Korolev was imprisoned in the Russian city of Kazan. For reasons that remain unknown, however, Korolev did not immediately leave the area to reunite with his family after his release. Instead, he stayed in Kazan, as a free man, for about a year. During this time, little is known about the details of his life and activities, other than that he appears to have continued work on technical projects, possibly related to rocketry. Then, in early August 1945, the United States made a choice that would send Korolev from Kazan back to Moscow and alter the course of his life forever.

A mushroom cloud rises over Hiroshima after the United States dropped an atomic bomb on the Japanese city, August 6, 1945.

On August 6 and 9, 1945, the United States launched the world's first (and to date only) nuclear attacks, against Japan, targeting the cities of Hiroshima and Nagasaki, effectively ending World War II. As the world stood in awe of the American weapons, Soviet Union leader Joseph Stalin rushed to prioritize his country's nuclear program. The relationship between the US and the USSR had quickly fallen apart at the end of the war in Europe, due to the ideological differences between the two countries. When intelligence revealed that von Braun was in American custody, Stalin knew that the US had a strategic military advantage. If the United States paired their nuclear weapon with one of the German engineer's rockets, would they be able to fire a nuclear warhead that would reach the USSR? Stalin could not allow that to happen. He needed a rocket that would carry a nuclear warhead to the US to defend the Soviet Union against an American attack. He also needed a brilliant engineer to build it. Fortunately, such a man had been right under his nose throughout the war, clinging to life in the Gulag.

One month after Japan's surrender to the United States, Stalin summoned Korolev to Moscow and, in a spectacular display of hypocrisy, offered him a job. Korolev accepted the assignment. He was to travel to Germany and study the V-2 rocket in order to build a replica for the Soviet Union. It's difficult to understand why Korolev would have accepted the offer, given the brutality he had endured. But it's possible to imagine his motivation as he boarded a plane for Germany. He was free, and grateful to be returning to the work he loved, regardless of the circumstances. With the newly bestowed civilian rank of lieutenant colonel in the Red Army, he arrived in Germany not long before von Braun departed for America. The two men never crossed paths, but it was the only time during their lives that they were in such close proximity to one another.

In Germany, Korolev borrowed a car, a dusty two-door Opel Olympia, and set off on his new assignment. How quickly his life was now changing, while every moment in prison had dragged on for an eternity. Confinement had made him paranoid and cautious. His health had also been severely compromised by life in prison. He developed a heart condition that remained with him for the rest of his life, and the damage to his jawbones made it difficult to fully open his mouth. They were physical reminders of what the Gulag had taken from him. So much time had been lost. What might he have accomplished during those stolen years? If the NKVD had never shown up at his door, could he have surpassed von Braun?

There was no time to regret such things. Korolev's duty was to complete his mission as ordered by Stalin. Building a copy of von Braun's rocket would never be enough for him, though. Korolev's secret dream was to build one of his own: a Soviet original that would be superior to anything designed by von Braun.

Korolev increased pressure on the gas pedal. The Opel responded, and the ruins of Germany blurred outside the window. The road ahead was unfamiliar, but Korolev took each curve as it came, holding a steady course toward his uncertain future.

. . .

The first time Soviet engineer and Red Army major Boris Chertok met Sergei Korolev, the two men were standing inside a lavish villa in the town of Bleicherode, not far from Nordhausen, where the Mittelwerk V-2 factory was located. Villa Frank had been home to Wernher von Braun for a time near the end of the war. Now it served as headquarters of the Institute RABE, an organization of Soviet engineers whose job was to collect V-2s and other rocket parts. Chertok was the group's chief.

Korolev carried himself like an officer, Chertok recalled, but "the absence of medals on his clean tunic immediately gave him away as a 'civilian' officer. His dark eyes, which had a sort of merry sparkle, looked at me with curiosity and attentiveness . . . I immediately noticed Korolev's high forehead and large head on his short neck, . . . There was something about him, like a boxer during a fight."

Chertok invited Korolev to sit and watched as "he sank into a deep armchair and, with obvious pleasure, stretched out his legs."

Chertok began the briefing. He detailed the progress of the Soviets' V-2 recovery project and noted that a number of von Braun's former associates remained in Germany. Fortunately for the Soviets, not everyone who worked with von Braun had wanted (or been invited) to enter the United States under Operation Paperclip. Some of those German technicians now worked for the Soviets, locating parts to help re-create the V-2. A few engines had been recovered, and firing tests were underway. Satisfied with the overview, Korolev thanked Chertok and departed. Chertok watched as Korolev took his place behind the wheel of the dirty Opel and drove away. He had permission to pass through every Soviet checkpoint in Germany and could drive the Opel anywhere he chose. Years later, Chertok recalled the day he watched the former Gulag prisoner reclaiming his freedom. "He wasn't yet forty years old. . . . But he had the right now to take something from life for himself."

CHAPTER 7

CONFISCATING THE SPOILS OF WAR

It should have been easy for the Soviets to locate materials to re-assemble V-2s. But when they had first arrived at Mittelwerk, most of the V-2 rockets and parts were already gone. The American army had been the first Allied power to discover Camp Dora and its adjacent Mittelwerk factory, and had helped themselves to enough material to fully assemble at least one hundred V-2s as well as hardware for other weapons. But the V-2 material didn't technically belong to the Americans. When the war ended, Germany and Berlin were divided into four occupational zones, each controlled by one of the four victors in Europe: the United States, Great Britain, France, and the Soviet Union. Mittelwerk was inside the Soviet zone. The United States realized that all the V-2 components within the mountain factory would fall under Soviet control. The contents would be enough to kick-start a rocket program for the USSR.

Given the sweeping political differences between the two temporary allies, the United States could not allow the Soviet Union to acquire V-2 technology. On April 11, 1945, the US Army undertook drastic measures to prevent it. Special Mission V-2 was a large-scale operation that removed enough documentation, material, and mechanical parts from Mittelwerk to fully assemble one hundred V-2 rockets. But the packing and loading of the parts required the specialized skills of those accustomed to working with machinery. The most qualified team was the army's 144th Ordnance Motor Vehicle Assembly Company, but it was stationed eight hundred miles away in Cherbourg, France. It would take the reinforcements almost a month to arrive, leaving precious little time to pack and load the confiscated material aboard railcars bound for Antwerp and then the United States.

With less than three weeks until the Soviets' scheduled takeover of the site, and the area surrounding Nordhausen, the 144th finally arrived on May 18 and received help from an unlikely source. There were already a number of V-2 assembly experts in the area: the surviving former prisoners of Camp Dora who had been forced to work inside the mountain cave. For a fair wage, the army hired 150 former Dora prisoners to assist in gathering the rocket materials and loading them aboard as many as 350 railcars for transport. While teams hurried to empty Mittelwerk of its hardware, phase two of Special Mission V-2 began.

Persistent rumors about a secret document archive belonging to von Braun and hidden near Nordhausen convinced intelligence officials that it likely existed. The US Army ordered twenty-five-year-old Major Robert Staver to find and confiscate the documents before the area fell under Soviet control.

US intelligence was right to believe the rumors. Hitler had ordered von Braun's rocket research destroyed to keep it out of the hands of the Allies as Germany fell. To protect his archive, von Braun had once again defied Hitler's orders. Two of his most trusted engineers, Dieter Huzel and Bernhard Tessmann, secretly transported fourteen tons of documents and schematics to an abandoned mine shaft in Dörnten, forty-eight miles north of Nordhausen. The men then dynamited the entrance, sealing the homemade vault behind an avalanche of rock.

Von Braun believed his documents could be used as valuable leverage against the Americans if he needed to further persuade them of his usefulness. He departed for the US under Operation Paperclip having never revealed their location.

Racing against the clock, Major Staver falsified a note suggesting that von Braun had ordered the disclosure of his archive's hiding place to the Americans. Staver presented the bogus statement to Walther Riedel and Karl Otto Fleischer, two former colleagues of von Braun's who likely knew the documents' secret location. Assuming the note was authentic, Fleischer revealed the location of the mine, and Staver took possession of von Braun's collection of papers.

On May 31, at nine thirty p.m., the last train, loaded with the life's work of Wernher von Braun, departed Mittelwerk just hours before the Soviets arrived.

With the Americans' shameless looting of both Mittelwerk and von Braun's secret document stash, the US expanded its technological advantage. It was a blow to the Soviets. Korolev's job was more difficult because he would have to start from scratch. His proud Russian upbringing and devotion to his country mattered more than this setback. He was driven and skilled, undaunted by the unique challenges presented by large-scale rocket projects. To successfully reverse engineer the V-2, he first needed to draft a new set of rocket schematics. Helmut Gröttrup, a former assistant to von Braun, was one of the engineers who had chosen to stay behind in Germany. In exchange for a good salary and comfortable accommodations for himself and his family, Gröttrup accepted a job working for the Soviets to help them build V-2s. Gröttrup and other associates of von Braun's were willing to disregard any concerns they may have had about working for the Soviets because they needed to feed their families in devasted postwar Germany. During negotiations, Gröttrup stipulated that he would not relocate to the Soviet Union with his wife and child, wanting to remain in Germany. The Soviets agreed to these terms with Gröttrup and the other Germans who worked for them.

Their new employers, however, maintained strict control over the new V-2 rocket program.

The Russians eventually realized that if they were going to establish a successful rocket production operation in their own country, they needed the Germans with them in the Soviet Union. Given the choice, the German engineers, especially Gröttrup, could refuse to leave. It was a risk that Soviet intelligence was unwilling to take.

On October 19, 1946, the Soviet special deputy for counterintelligence, Colonel Ivan Serov, arrived in Germany. In his memoir, Boris Chertok described a meeting between Serov and the Soviet engineers working at Institute RABE. Serov wanted lists of valuable German specialists who could be useful working in the Soviet Union. These specialists, Chertok wrote, "would be taken to the Soviet Union regardless of their own wishes." Serov reportedly said, "We will allow the Germans to take all their things with them, even furniture. We don't have much of that. As far as family members, they can go if they wish."

Then Serov laid out his plan. "No action is required of you except for a farewell banquet. Get them good and drunk—it will be easier to endure the trauma." Chertok struggled to comply with the order. He had worked alongside the Germans. He knew they were about to be tricked into leaving Germany and forced to move to the Soviet Union. "It was difficult," Chertok wrote, "to seriously discuss future projects knowing that one night soon, they and their families would be 'seized.'" Korolev had reservations about the plan as well and reportedly remarked that the Soviets "must have a little more self-respect." He knew what it felt like to be torn from one's home in the middle of the night.

On the evening of October 22, the Soviets hosted a banquet at a local restaurant. Alcohol flowed freely at the bar for the Germans. Serov and his men remained sober. An extravagant table and festive lighting added to the celebratory atmosphere. "Fruit was in absolute abundance," one attendee recalled, although it was nearly non-existent in postwar Germany. It was a huge feast, another diner said, but the only thing to drink was "vodka, vodka, vodka." Around one a.m. the party ended. The well-fed and thoroughly intoxicated Germans were driven home.

At around four o'clock in the morning, the phone rang at the Gröttrups' house and Helmut's wife, Irmgard, answered. "The Russians are at the front door. We're going to be taken away," a voice said.

Irmgard believed it was a prank until the Russians began arriving by the hundreds. Their promise to the Gröttrup family, and other Germans who worked for them, was broken. They were told to gather their belongings and board trains for the Soviet Union. Most did not resist. "The dazed, half-asleep Germans didn't immediately grasp why they needed to go to work in the Soviet Union at four o'clock in the morning," Chertok wrote. "But the discipline, order, and the unquestioning subordination to authority that had been drilled into them and under which the entire German people had lived for many decades did the trick. An order [was] an order." Approximately five thousand skilled German rocket specialists and their families were abducted and transported to the Soviet Union, where they would work with Korolev to build rockets for the Russians.

CHAPTER 8

BACK TO THE USSR

By February 1947, after more than a year of studying recovered V-2s in Germany, Sergei Korolev was back in the USSR. When he and his team first saw their future missile factory, a former air defense site in Podlipki, a suburb of Moscow, Chertok recalled, "we were horrified." The Soviet rocket engineers had grown accustomed to the organized and well-maintained facilities they had left behind in Germany. The facility looked like something out of the Stone Age. "There was dirt and primitive equipment . . . [that] had been ransacked," Chertok wrote. The recently deported Germans lived in overcrowded barracks and tents in and around Moscow. World War II had devastated the Soviet Union. As many as 1,700 cities had been destroyed and approximately twenty-seven million people were dead. Rebuilding the country would take years, but defense of the Soviet homeland could not wait.

Korolev's relationship with his wife was in equally bad shape. The years of separation during his imprisonment in the Gulag had driven a wedge between the once-happy couple. They would eventually divorce in 1948 after Korolev began an affair with another woman while he was still married to Ksenia. Korolev's betrayal infuriated his eleven-year-old daughter, Natalia, who blamed her father for destroying their family. The rift in their relationship lasted nearly a decade.

While his personal life crumbled, Korolev and his Russian/German staff began the difficult task of building a production system for Soviet rocket manufacturing. They worked long hours in poorly heated facilities with leaky roofs. The engineers didn't have worktables for their drawings, so they repurposed overturned equipment boxes as desks. With slide rules and pencils balanced between frozen fingers, engineers meticulously re-created V-2 schematics and calculated by hand the brain-bending mathematics required to make a rocket fly.

In April, Stalin summoned Korolev to Moscow for a progress report on the emerging V-2 project. Korolev was nervous. He hoped to convince the Soviet leader that it was time to move beyond the replication of the V-2 and build an original Russian-made rocket.

Korolev later recalled the events in a letter to Ksenia. When he arrived at the meeting, the chamber was filled with at least a hundred high-ranking Soviet officials. Stalin paced the room with a pipe in his mouth. He "did not offer his hand." The dictator questioned Korolev about rockets. He wanted to know if planes were better suited for the deployment of weapons. Korolev responded by emphasizing the superiority of rockets over airplanes. Stalin listened, "silently at first, hardly taking his pipe out of his mouth," then interrupted the designer with "terse questions."

Korolev patiently answered them, then swallowed his anxiety and pressed ahead with his agenda for the meeting. He told Stalin that his design team was capable of building a better rocket than von Braun's, one with a longer range than the already obsolete V-2. Wouldn't it be a better use of time and resources to create an original Russian-made rocket? Stalin disagreed, because he was too preoccupied with the development of an atomic bomb. He insisted that the engineer focus on replicating von Braun's proven V-2. Disappointed, Korolev accepted the decision. He would bide his time and wait for another opportunity to change Stalin's mind.

In late summer of that same year, the Soviets began building a bare-bones launch facility to test Korolev's V-2 replica. The site was a remote and barren desert less than a hundred miles southeast of the town of Volgograd. Conditions at the Kapustin Yar test range were even more wretched than the cold and leaky workshop outside Moscow. The desolate area offered no human comforts, but its isolation made it ideal for testing unpredictable rockets. Every basic necessity had to be imported, including food, water, and shelter. Engineers, workers, and their families lived onsite in railcars. They would freeze through subzero winters and swelter during blazing-hot summers. The sand teemed with tarantulas and venomous snakes. But the remote facility was far enough away from populated areas to to maintain secrecy around the rocket project, while also safeguarding civilian lives if one of Korolev's test rockets flew off course. Korolev couldn't have known that thousands of miles away in an American desert, the V-2's inventor, Wernher von Braun, was equally frustrated by a government that insisted on tying his hands. Like Korolev, von Braun's dream of developing a brand-new rocket was on hold as he waited patiently for his shot.

CHAPTER 9

SPACE COWBOYS

It was another hot, dry day in Fort Bliss, Texas. Thirty-five-year-old Wernher von Braun squinted into the sun and watched as an object spiraled toward him. Should he stand his ground or get out of the way? Von Braun sprinted forward, raised his arm, and smashed the volleyball. It whizzed over the net and was unreturned. He smiled. It must have felt good to win, because life in the US proved disappointing at first. His team had not been assigned to any new rocket development projects.

Since their arrival in 1945, they had worked almost daily with the Americans, teaching them to fly the confiscated V-2s that had been shipped to the US from the Mittelwerk tunnels in Nordhausen.

The Germans began referring to themselves as "POPs" (prisoners of peace) and found creative ways to pass the time when they were not working. During the day, they played volleyball, gardened, or completed simple construction projects, such as building furniture for their austere barracks. At night, their quarters looked and sounded more like a college fraternity house than a military post. The engineers staged elaborate competitive battles against each other with fire hoses, sandbags, water bombs, and pillows.

Von Braun (black pants) enjoys a game of volleyball at Fort Bliss, Texas, in 1947.

As more time passed, the group became increasingly restless with the baby-step pace of the American military. "Frankly, we were disappointed with what we found in this country during our first year or so," von Braun said years later. "We were distrusted aliens living in what for us was a desolate region of a foreign land. . . . Nobody seemed to be much interested in work that smelled of weapons, now [that] the war was over and spaceflight was a concept bordering on the ridiculous."

At Peenemünde, the Germans had fired as many as two missiles per day; now they were lucky if they fired two in a month. Von Braun's dream of kicking off an American space program seemed as unlikely as a rainy day in the Texas desert. He realized that he and the other German rocketeers had been spoiled with the best tools and equipment money could buy. "We had been coddled," von Braun later said. "Here they were counting pennies." Some members of his team wondered if surrendering to the United States had been a bad idea. They wanted to build new rockets, not tinker with technology they had already perfected. When tensions escalated within the group, von Braun implored them to be patient and remember the reason they had come to America: it was the first stop on their way to the moon.

The German Operation Paperclip rocketeers assembled at Fort Bliss, Texas.

It was also a way to help their families. Under their temporary contracts with the army, the engineers earned a small salary, most of which they sent home to their loved ones who were still living in devastated postwar Germany.

Despite their frustrations, the engineers were proving themselves as valuable long-term national security assets. However, their contracts were only for six months. Operation Paperclip had been a temporary project, not a permanent immigration program. So the government began taking steps to transform the wartime operation into a permanent path to citizenship. Some of Paperclip's most valuable participants, like von Braun and members of his Fort Bliss group, received new contracts, extending their stay for as long as two years. Since they would be in the country on a more permanent basis, the time had come to reveal Operation Paperclip to the American people.

In early 1946, the War Department issued a series of carefully worded statements about the nature of Operation Paperclip, without disclosing its most scandalous detail: that some of the program's alumni had been ardent Nazis, or in the case of von Braun, members of Hitler's SS. The War Department hoped a controlled release of information over time would minimize any backlash. The broad outlines of the secret program gradually became public knowledge. Americans learned the project's name and its stated purpose of leveraging German science to benefit national defense. The identities of some of the participants, including von Braun's, were released as well. When the *El Paso Times* ran the story, it called von Braun's team "the brains behind Hitler's boasted 'secret weapon,' the V-2 rocket," declaring, "Now they have turned their skill over to their former enemies." No attempt was made to hide von Braun's membership in the Nazi Party. It would have been too difficult to conceal, given his position as the V-2's designer.

The War Department press releases stressed that the Germans had been thoroughly vetted (which we now know wasn't entirely true). Some Americans, at the time, were understandably skeptical. Detroit congressman John D. Dingell was outraged that the United States government would consider partnering with the Germans. "I have never thought that we were so poor mentally in this country that we have to go and import those Nazi killers to help us prepare for the defense of our country. A German is a Nazi and a Nazi is a German. The terms are synonymous," he said. Dingell's comments echoed the lingering anger many Americans felt against Germany after the war and their fear that war criminals would be allowed into the US. And while not every German citizen or participant in Operation Paperclip was a "killer," as Dingell described, some of the Paperclip scientists, engineers, and technicians had been Nazi officers and/or zealous believers in Hitler's cause. In the case of von Braun, he was a Nazi officer who knew that concentration camp prisoners at Mittelwerk assembled his rockets, but chose not to allow that fact to interfere with his ambitious plans.

Meanwhile, V-2 launch days at the nearby White Sands Missile

Range in White Sands, New Mexico, became a spectator sport. Visitors drove from miles around, their cars and trucks streaming along Route 70 to watch in awe as the powerful V-2 ripped off the sand and into the sky. Curious onlookers parked on the roadside, and passengers craned their necks to catch a glimpse of the future.

These V-2 test flights, known as Project Fire-Ball, were milestones in American rocket research. Between 1946 and 1951, nearly seventy V-2 rockets were fired. Instead of explosives, instruments flew inside some of the V-2 nose cones, measuring temperature, pressure, and cosmic rays in the upper atmosphere. Nose cone cameras captured photographs of the Earth's atmosphere, a precursor to future weather satellite technology.

Although the government continued to ignore von Braun's early proposals for a space program, another of his proposals received an enthusiastic "Yes!" Von Braun was in love with a beautiful young woman named Maria von Quistorp, his eighteen-year-old first cousin, who lived in Germany. Marriages between first cousins are less common in American society, but historically were not unusual among European aristocracy. Von Braun's feelings for Maria had not diminished in the two years since he had last seen her. "I had secretly hoped for her hand if ever the world settled down," he wrote. In a letter to his father, Magnus, von Braun asked him to find out if Maria still had feelings for him. The elder von Braun, eager to arrange the marriage for his son, immediately went to Maria. With the "subtlety of a bulldozer," he blurted out, "I am supposed to find out if you will marry Wernher. What shall I tell him?" She wrote to von Braun in the US, "I'd never thought of marrying anyone else." Given von Braun's immense value to the United States government, he required special permission to travel to Germany for the ceremony. The army worried that the Soviets could attempt to kidnap him. To ensure his safety, an army escort was provided for the entire trip. The couple was married in Landshut, Germany, on March 1, 1947.

When von Braun returned to the US with his new wife, he was welcomed with a harsh reminder of the secret past he wanted to keep buried. A war crimes investigator was in El Paso to interview members of his team. Nazis were standing trial in Dachau, Germany, for crimes committed at the Dachau concentration camp and the Mittelbau-Dora concentration camp in central Germany, where the Mittelwerk V-2 factory was located. As the general director of the secret rocket manufacturing plant, Georg Rickhey stood among the accused. He was a Nazi working as an administrator at Mittelwerk, tasked with organizing the underground V-2 operation. It was a tough job. The brutality of the SS made it nearly impossible to maintain a prison labor force, because so many of them died.

A number of von Braun's team members in El Paso were deposed for Rickhey's trial, but for reasons still unknown, von Braun was not interviewed at the time. Those who were questioned, including von Braun's longtime colleague Arthur Rudolph, played it close to the vest and provided a highly sanitized version of conditions at Mittelwerk to minimize Rickhey's role. They stressed that he was little more than a figurehead and questioned the fairness of blaming Rickhey when it was the SS and their appointed guards inside the factory who actually carried out the atrocities against the prisoners. Those who were interviewed fell back on the tried-and-true tactic of scapegoating the SS, thereby deflecting attention from their own complicity in the war's atrocities. The bloody reputation of Hitler's elite guard made it easy to assume they were to blame.

Von Braun was later called as a witness for Rickhey's defense. Citing security concerns, the US Army refused to allow von Braun to travel to Germany to testify in person. Instead, he submitted written sworn testimony. Like Rudolph and the other rocket group members, von Braun echoed denials of Rickhey's responsibilty in the Mittelwerk operation. He wrote: "I am not acquainted with the formal position which Mr. Rickhey had in the corporation as well as with his duties, competences and authority. However, I do know that Mr. Rickhey had very little influence in the *actual* deciding powers that determined the activities of the Mittelwerk." By December, the Dachau-Nordhausen trial ended and Rickhey was acquitted. This brush with the war crimes trial reminded von Braun and his group that their favorable position with the United States government was not guaranteed. Careless conversations about their lives and work during the war could invite more questions from their American hosts—questions that could cost them—and especially von Braun—everything.

For thousands of years, the swastika was an emblem of health, well-being, and peace. The Nazis adopted the symbol, twisting it into an icon of hate. In this 1947 photo of von Braun (third from right) and company, the swastika appears on the store's sign, ironically, in its original ancient form.

Kapustin Yar Test Range

SEPTEMBER 21, 1949

While von Braun waited for the US government to give him and his team a meaningful assignment, in the USSR Sergei Korolev was beginning to make progress. After two years of painstakingly re-creating V-2 schematics, his team of engineers had built and launched a replica of von Braun's rocket. This milestone prompted Stalin to approve the design and development of the first *original* Russian rocket, known as the R-2. On the launchpad at Kapustin Yar, it was ready for flight. The sixty-foot, twenty-ton vehicle had an improved guidance system and achieved twice the range of von

Braun's V-2. Korolev's biggest innovation had been the R-2's detachable nose cone. Once the rocket's fuel was spent, the tank fell away. Now lighter, it could travel farther and faster. The military planned to pack the nose cone with a bomb, but Korolev had something else in mind. He wanted his R-2 to carry and release a satellite into Earth orbit. But he hid this secret aspiration from the NKVD, who watched him closely. If they suspected Korolev was working on anything other than national defense, he could be arrested again.

Korolev watched the R-2 lift from the pad, slowly at first, then gaining speed and arcing into the sky. It landed 370 miles from the launch site. His dream of launching a satellite was within reach.

As von Braun continued to wait for his chance to build a new rocket in the United States, he had no reason to wonder what the Soviets were up to. Knowledge of Korolev's success with the R-2 would have made bad matters worse. Von Braun's patience with the American army was exhausted. For five years he and his team had dutifully fulfilled the terms of their contracts. They had gradually educated themselves about American culture and improved their English-speaking skills, though von Braun's accent was now tinged with a distinct Texas twang. The US Army had the best German engineers at their disposal, not to mention von Braun's original rocket plans and schematics, and yet they did nothing. "We can dream about rockets and the Moon until Hell freezes over," he vented to his colleague Dr. Adolf Thiel. "Unless the *people* understand it and the man who pays the bill is behind it, no dice." Wernher von Braun decided to take his plea directly to the American people.

With the army's permission, he gave passionate presentations to local civic groups and clubs. He talked to anyone who would listen. When he described satellites orbiting the Earth and the possibility of travel to other planets, awestruck audiences responded with standing ovations. Concerns about his role in the war faded as the charismatic von Braun spun a romantic vision of space travel—a future he assured them was within reach. A future he knew with absolute certainty he could deliver.

And while the German engineer shared his message of progress with the American public, the secretive Soviets were about to deliver a public message of their own: they had become a nuclear power.

CHAPTER 10

THE COLD WAR

On August 29, 1949, Soviet nuclear physicists unleashed a shock wave of paranoia and fear on America with the successful testing of their first atomic bomb. Until that point, most Americans perceived the Soviet Union as a backward country that had been devastated by World War II. However, while it was still recovering from the war, and millions of Soviets were desperately poor, the population also included well-educated people and many folks who fell somewhere in between. How had they produced an atomic bomb? As it turned out, they had some help.

The Soviet Union had enlisted the assistance of an average-looking, thirtysomething married American couple, Julius and Ethel Rosenberg. The pair became communists sometime during the early 1930s. Their zealous belief in the cause led them to become spies for the Soviet Union, who wanted them to steal intelligence on America's atomic bomb.

Ethel's brother, David Greenglass, worked as a machinist at the Los Alamos National Laboratory in New Mexico, where the bomb was being developed under the code name Manhattan Project. With access to classified bomb-building intelligence inside the lab, Greenglass took mental notes of what he saw and drew pictures from memory. When it was time to pass along the stolen information, Julius Rosenberg set up a secret protocol to help Greenglass identify his contact. Rosenberg gave him half a box top from a container of Jell-O. His contact, Rosenberg said, would be carrying the other half. Whether or not the Rosenbergs directly contributed to the Soviets' acquisition of a nuclear bomb remains a matter of debate. But it was enough to convict them both of treason. The couple was executed in 1953.

The threat of nuclear war did not die with the Rosenbergs. The world now had two nuclear superpowers, each one ready to defend itself using the deadliest weapon ever created. The stakes had never been higher, and the United States and the USSR began competing in an arms race, expanding their arsenals with ever larger, more destructive nuclear weapons. They foolishly believed that the creation of more weapons of mass destruction was the best way to defend their countries. This potentially catastrophic game of brinkmanship was an aggressive political tactic in which the rival countries deliberately forced each other to the edge of confrontation. The goal of brinkmanship was for one country to gain a strategic advantage over its rival. The country with the most dangerous weapon won the upper hand, at least for a while, until its enemy developed a new weapon that surpassed it. But this arms race was a pointless exercise, of course. It didn't matter how many bombs were built; in all-out nuclear war, everyone would lose. Ironically, the threat of mutually assured destruction prevented the Soviet Union and the United States from launching a nuclear attack. This tense and threatening period became known as the Cold War.

Earl Reichert of Battle Creek, Michigan, and other Americans like him, weren't taking any chances. They sought peace of mind by constructing bomb shelters in their backyards. Stockpiled with food and water, these underground fortresses would theoretically help families survive a nuclear attack. "War will come sooner or later," Reichert said. "And we want to be protected against bomb-blast and radiation." Reichert's doomsday refuge was a twenty-by-forty-foot fortress made of thirty-one feet of solid concrete and sixteen-inch steel beams and buried beneath four feet of earth. "You buy life insurance but no one benefits from it until you're dead," he said. "This kind of insurance keeps you alive."

American television networks warned about a possible Soviet nuclear attack. A commercial featuring a friendly animated turtle named Bert reminded kids to "duck and cover" when they saw the flash of an atomic blast. It was absurd to think that all it would take to survive a nuclear bomb was to duck beneath a table and cover one's head. Nevertheless, in schools across the country, American students regularly practiced diving under their desks in mandatory duck-and-cover drills.

Schoolchildren participate in a duck-and-cover drill in their classroom during the 1950s.

As tensions mounted between America and the USSR, their symbolic differences were about to erupt on the ground in Korea.

During World War II, Korea had belonged to the empire of Japan. When the Allies defeated the Japanese, Korea was divided into two zones: the Soviet-occupied north and the US-occupied south. On June 25, 1950, North Korea invaded South Korea, sparking the Korean War. The United States and the Soviet Union were both involved as supporters on opposite sides of the fight but did not engage each other directly. It was a proxy war between the two superpowers—one not taking place on their own soil—that lasted three years, killing as many as two and a half million people.

As fear of communist expansion increased with the escalating war in Korea, the German engineers who had been cooling their heels in the Texas desert became essential to America's Cold War defense strategy. Congress authorized more military spending, and the Pentagon approved a plan to develop a nuclear missile capable of reaching the Soviet Union. A new Army Ordnance Guided Missile Center was announced. It would be headquartered at an abandoned World War II chemical weapons facility in Huntsville, Alabama, called Redstone Arsenal. After five years of waiting, von Braun and his team were finally getting their first new rocket project, one that would help defend the United States against the USSR. It wasn't a spaceship, but it was a sign of confidence in von Braun and his team's ability. His entire group would have to be quickly relocated to Alabama.

There was only one problem: those pesky paper clips attached to the original file of every German who had been brought to the United States outside of the established immigration system. Before any of von Braun's team could move to Huntsville and begin their official employment with the army, they each had to reenter the country *legally* for the first time. Getting their paperwork in order was also essential because the Germans would be allowed to apply for citizenship after they had legally been in the United States for five years.

One by one, the engineers reentered the United States using the same strange procedure. When it was von Braun's turn, he climbed aboard an El Paso streetcar, escorted by an American officer in civilian clothes, paid the five-cent fare, and and rode into Ciudad Juárez, across the US-Mexican border from El Paso, where everything had been prearranged with the Mexican and American officers. At the American consulate, he submitted the necessary paperwork and paid a fee of eighteen dollars in cash. His paperwork was stamped and the two men returned to the border. When the streetcar neared the American side, von Braun was asked to state where he had come from. He answered, as required, "Mexico," and his papers were stamped again. With that, von Braun had established his legal

IMMIGRATION CONTROVERSY

In the 1950s, von Braun's privileged status as a contract employee of the United States Army and his value to national defense helped clear red tape to facilitate his entry into the country. Today, immigrants without the kind of privilege von Braun benefited from aren't as fortunate. They endure risky, sometimes deadly journeys across hundreds or thousands of miles, hoping to enter America and build a better future. Tragically, many of them die trying.

presence in the United States. After five years, he and his Operation Paperclip team would be eligible to apply for American citizenship. Recalling the momentous day, von Braun later said that the five-cent streetcar ride to Juárez "was the most valuable nickel [he] ever spent!" Back at Fort Bliss, he packed his bags, ready to set off toward his new home, Huntsville, Alabama, where he and his team would be civil service employees of the United States government.

CHAPTER 11

WELCOME TO THE WATERCRESS CAPITAL OF THE WORLD!

1949

The first time Huntsville mayor Robert Searcy saw the group of German engineers, he thought they were "a bunch of crazy rocket men." The quiet and isolated town of fifteen thousand people was tucked into the Appalachian foothills of northern Alabama. Some of the locals greeted the engineers with curious smiles and friendly handshakes. Other times, the "outsiders" drew suspicion from those who were hesitant to trust newcomers.

The team took it all in stride. They had finally escaped the dry, dull Texas desert and arrived in a lush green landscape that reminded them of Germany. The self-proclaimed "Watercress Capital of the World" earned its title, as fields of watercress and cotton stretched around it for miles. Von Braun loved it all. Maria had given birth to their first daughter, Iris Careen, before they left Texas, and Huntsville was a beautiful place to raise his growing family.

The team settled in at the Redstone Arsenal, now the home of the Army Ordnance Guided Missile Center. Von Braun was named project director of America's first ballistic missile, the Redstone rocket. The Redstone was essentially a much bigger V-2 and would become the first large-scale missile powered by liquid fuel.

CLASSIFIED INTELLIGENCE DOSSIER
TOP SECRET
DO NOT COPY!

Subject: Redstone missile

Nickname: "Old Reliable"

Description: Single-stage rocket.

Range: 200–250 miles

Length: 69 feet

Weight: 39 tons

First successful test launch: August 20, 1953

Payload capacity: up to four-megaton thermonuclear warhead

The historic Redstone rocket test stand at the Marshall Space Flight Center in Huntsville, Alabama.

As the German team set up shop in Huntsville, the details of von Braun's connection to Mittelwerk remained hidden. No one—not the media, the government, or the American public—was digging around in his past. The Soviets had a nuclear weapon, and safeguarding the United States with a nuclear missile was the national priority. The Germans were perceived as smart, capable technologists who were willing to lend a helping hand when America needed it most.

In exchange, von Braun and his team were rewarded with the opportunity to rebuild their lives and careers. As German rocket specialist Ernst Stuhlinger put it, they were finally "free to move around, to rent or to buy houses, to join churches and civil organizations . . . and to eventually become real citizens of the United States of America."

It was a privileged statement coming from a man like Stuhlinger. He, like the rest of the Germans, was white, which automatically made him and his German colleagues part of the privileged white class in the rural South of the 1950s. Local banks offered the Germans affordable housing loans. Without assets or a credit history, they could borrow as much as $400. African Americans who had been born and raised in the South could be denied those same privileges for no other reason than the color of their skin. Throughout the South, Black people lived in fear of the Ku Klux Klan, which terrorized and murdered them at will. Like the Nazis in Germany, the Klan traded in hate speech, threatened, and killed, all in the name of ensuring racial purity. American troops had fought this kind of hatred in World War II while at home, their fellow Black Americans were dying from the same type of bigotry.

Downtown Huntsville, Alabama, 1946.

•　•　•

As Huntsville adjusted to its newest residents, development of the Redstone rocket progressed. The Germans knew if it could carry a nuclear weapon, it could also launch a satellite into orbit. Von Braun understood he would need the ongoing support of the American people to pull it off. He remained committed to his speaking engagements, with the unwavering goal of building support for space exploration.

His timing couldn't have been better. America's latest obsession was science fiction. Futuristic films, comics, and novels dominated movie theaters and bookshelves, with titles like *Destination Moon* and *The Man from Planet X*. These far-flung fantasies offered an escape from the terrifying reality of communism and the Cold War threat. Children formed rocket clubs, turning family garages into workshops and neighborhood playgrounds into launchpads. America was dreaming of space travel.

The Space Prophet

In 1952, *Collier's*, a popular American magazine with no less than four million subscribers, planned a series of articles about the future of technology and space travel and invited von Braun to contribute to the series. His first article, "Crossing the Last Frontier," debuted in March of that year. It was lavishly illustrated with full-color paintings depicting the high-tech future that von Braun described: a large 250-foot-wide wheel-shaped Earth-orbiting satellite, inhabited by people, that would travel over four miles per second, twenty times the speed of sound.

American readers were transfixed by von Braun's vision of a space age, but satellites were just the beginning. "From this platform, a trip to the moon itself will be just a step," he wrote. The spectacular near future described by von Braun read like a thrilling science-fiction story, but it was real. Space travel was possible! It was all there in the pages of *Collier's*, and closer than anyone had ever imagined, thanks to Wernher von Braun.

All of this would cost money, of course—huge sums. And von Braun knew it. His earliest experiences with rockets in Germany had taught him that money was the real fuel that made a rocket fly. He did not shy away from the truth of the project's cost. "The job would take ten years and cost twice as much as the atomic bomb," he wrote. But "if we can do it, we can not only preserve the peace, but we can take a long step toward uniting mankind."

The tone of the article was optimistic, but the *Collier's* editors delivered an ominous warning to their readers in its introduction. "The US must immediately . . . secure for the West 'space superiority.' If we do not, somebody else will. That somebody else very probably would be the Soviet Union." And that was the real threat: that its enemy, the USSR, would beat the United States. Utopian dreams of world peace and cooperation in space captured American minds, hearts, and imaginations, but in truth, prestige and power were the endgame for both rival governments.

CHAPTER 12

THE INTERCONTINENTAL BALLISTIC MISSILE (ICBM)

One year later, on March 6, 1953, the *New York Times* declared: "Stalin Dies after 29-Year Rule. His Successor Not Announced. US Watchful, Eisenhower Says." At the age of seventy-three, Stalin had suffered an apparent stroke and related brain hemorrhage. By September 1953, Nikita Khrushchev had risen to power and was named first secretary of the Communist Party.

How would the loss of their leader impact the Soviet Union? Believe it or not, some Russians wept. In fact, Sergei Korolev was one of the millions of former Gulag prisoners who mourned Stalin's death. As illogical as it seems, many Russians did not hold Stalin personally responsible for their suffering. They actually looked up to him.

THE INTERCONTINENTAL BALLISTIC MISSILE (ICBM)

As for Korolev, he had continued to admire the Soviet leader. It had not been Joseph Stalin who knocked on his door that terrible evening and ripped him from his family. It had been the secret police, the NKVD. Perhaps it was easier to believe Stalin was ignorant than to accept the ugly truth that the leader of the Soviet Union had been a monster.

Korolev did not speak openly about his time in prison, though the long-term effects of torture occasionally surfaced in the stoic rocketeer, especially at mealtime. He gobbled his food and would wipe his plate clean with a piece of bread. His longing for food and warmth now satisfied, a new hunger took its place. Korolev's desire to succeed with his rockets was insatiable. He was working on a new project. The most ambitious of any he had undertaken thus far, and one that accelerated the science of rocket engineering. He could not reclaim the years he had lost in the Gulag, but if he succeeded, maybe they would not have been for nothing.

The new rocket, the R-7 Semyorka—from the Russian word for "seven"—would be the most powerful missile in the world, standing as tall as a nine-story building and weighing 280 tons.

It had to be that big. Soviet nuclear physicists were poised to build a three-to-five-megaton thermonuclear device. The R-7 rocket would need to carry the massive warhead over five thousand miles, far enough to reach a major US city. In designing a rocket with the capacity to deliver a weapon of mass destruction of that size to its target, Korolev was also creating the world's first intercontinental ballistic missile (ICBM), a rocket powerful enough to travel between two continents. The revolutionary design was the dawn of a new age in warfare, making it possible to launch a rocket attack against enemies thousands of miles away.

Korolev's R-7 was composed of two sections, or *stages*. The first stage had four liquid fuel engines that supplied the massive thrust required to boost the vehicle off the ground at launch. When the first stage's fuel supply was spent, the engines fell away. All that remained was the second stage, now lighter and able to fly farther because the first stage had been detached.

INTERCONTINENTAL BALLISTIC MISSILES

With his invention of the ICBM, Korolev forever changed modern warfare by making the world a much smaller place. This dark by-product of his scientific legacy is a global threat, particularly from countries like North Korea, where the isolated communist dictatorship is working to become a nuclear power. It routinely tests ballistic and intercontinental ballistic missiles in an attempt to threaten and intimidate other nations, like its neighbor, South Korea, and the United States.

Subject: R-7 missile

Nickname: "Semyorka" (Seven)

Description: Two-stage rocket and the world's first intercontinental ballistic missile (ICBM).

Range: 5,000 miles

Length: 102 feet

Weight: 280 tons

First successful test launch: August 21, 1957

Payload capacity: up to five-ton nuclear warhead

R-7 rocket (Semyorka).

Just as von Braun had bigger plans for his Redstone rocket, Korolev wanted more for his R-7. He knew that in order for an object to break free of Earth's gravity, it needed to travel at a velocity close to four miles per second, roughly the speed required for his R-7 to fly halfway around the world. To achieve such velocity, the rocket needed powerful engines. To build them, Korolev called on the

Soviet Union's greatest rocket engine designer: Valentin Petrovich Glushko.

Yes, *that* Valentin Glushko. The same man Korolev had been

thrown into the Gulag for defending against NKVD accusations. Glushko, like Korolev, had shown early promise as a bright boy with a vivid imagination. He was born in Ukraine in 1908. By the age of twelve, he, too, read Jules Verne novels and dreamed of space travel. Glushko studied math and physics at Leningrad State University. By 1930, he was working on electric rocket engine research.

Russian rocket engine designer
Valentin Petrovich Glushko.

Swept up in Stalin's purges, Glushko had been arrested in 1938 but was not sentenced to a labor camp like Kolyma. He had been more fortunate than Korolev. Glushko served his entire sentence in one of the sharashka prisons for technically skilled workers. He was among the group of engineers, including Korolev, who were suddenly released from prison near the end of World War II. He, too, was dispatched to

Soviet-occupied Germany, where he aided in the study and recovery of German rocket technology, specializing in engines.

Reliable accounts confirm that Korolev and Glushko had an amicable working relationship, despite their complicated history and imprisonment. They even exchanged Christmas cards. Although there was constant bickering over small details, a "general atmosphere of truly creative enthusiasm prevailed," one engineer recalled.

Inside the emerging Soviet space program, however, loyalty would become an increasingly rare commodity as ambition and bitter rivalry fueled the obsessive quest for spaceships.

CHAPTER 13

A ROCKET MAN IN TOMORROWLAND

1954

While Korolev and Glushko worked together to design an inter-continental ballistic missile that could deliver a weapon of mass destruction to the United States, Walt Disney was trying to build the happiest place on Earth in Anaheim, California. The massive theme park would revolve around his animated characters and films. But the beloved Mickey Mouse creator needed money to finance the project. So he struck a deal with the ABC television network. In exchange for the network's funding Disneyland's construction, Walt Disney would produce *Disneyland*, a weekly televison program with segments correlating to the park's four areas: Adventureland, Frontierland, Fantasyland, and Tomorrowland. Disney had ideas for the first three programs, but "Tomorrowland" proved difficult to conceptualize.

One of Walt Disney's animators, Ward Kimball, told him how impressed he had been with von Braun's articles in *Collier's*. The two men agreed that Wernher von Braun was the perfect person to educate the country about the future of space travel in the "Tomorrowland" program for ABC. It was the chance von Braun had been waiting for. The Disney program provided an ideal platform to rally support for spaceflight. *Collier's* had made von Braun increasingly popular. He had become so famous, in fact, that he hired a Hollywood talent agent to manage his new role as America's favorite spaceflight celebrity. When von Braun accepted Disney's offer, his talent agent brokered the deal.

Walt Disney and von Braun, 1954.

On March 9, 1955, Walt Disney made Wernher von Braun a household name before a record-setting viewing audience of forty million Americans. The articulate engineer explained in clear and accessible terms how a rocket ship crewed by highly trained astronauts could leave Earth and explore outer space. His expertise and convincing delivery provided an escape for Americans who feared communists lurking at the borders and nuclear bombs falling from the sky. Von Braun and Walt Disney gave people what they wanted most: hope for a better tomorrow. In the process, the rocket man became a star.

Those watching von Braun on television or reading about him in newspapers and magazines had no knowledge of his connection to Mittelwerk, or that he had been an officer in Hitler's SS. His membership in the Nazi Party was not a secret, but von Braun was gifted at obscuring the questionable aspects of his past, reassuring Americans that he'd only ever been devoted to his rockets. He had never been an extremist, like Himmler, who, von Braun reminded them, had once arrested him. As for membership in the party, it had been nothing more than a distasteful administrative formality required in the pursuit of his life's work. Although von Braun had worked for Hitler, he had chosen to use his considerable technical skill to benefit the people of the United States. Many Americans no longer saw the inventor of the deadly V-2 when they looked at von Braun. Here was a smart, media-savvy genius, with an easy smile and a way with words, who appeared on television literally promising them the moon. There was no incentive to pry into von Braun's past when the technological future he promised was so thrilling.

Von Braun took the oath of American citizenship one month later in the Huntsville High School auditorium with his wife, Maria, and thirty-eight of the German rocket experts and their families. Von Braun called it "one of the proudest and most significant days of my life."

Von Braun's Petition for Naturalization bears his signature and paved the way for him to become a US citizen.

Cloudy with a Chance of Spy Satellites

President Dwight D. Eisenhower had no idea what the Soviets were up to, but he feared the worst. "Since the advent of nuclear weapons, it seems clear that there is no longer any alternative to peace, if there is to be a happy and well world," he said. The decorated veteran had served as supreme commander of Allied forces in Europe during World War II. Now he was leading his country through the Cold War against the Soviet Union. Eisenhower believed military reconnaissance—spying—was the best way to protect America from the Soviet Union. After Russian nuclear physicists successfully tested the country's first thermonuclear bomb in August 1953—a 400-kiloton weapon (the Nagasaki bomb was 20 kilotons)— he worried about a surprise nuclear attack on the United States. Eisenhower remembered the bombing of Pearl Harbor by the Japanese. Kamikaze suicide pilots attacked, killing 2,335 military personnel and 68 civilians on December 7, 1941, drawing America into World War II.

The president feared a future Pearl Harbor–style nuclear confrontation. In early 1954, he approved illegal airplane surveillance of the Soviet Union. The low-altitude flights were dangerous, and pilots could be shot down by the Soviets if they were spotted. The Cold War was a new conflict that demanded new strategies. Eisenhower needed a better way to spy on the USSR from higher altitudes. For advice, he turned to another president.

Technological Capabilities Panel (TCP)

That same year, James Killian, president of the Massachusetts Institute of Technology (MIT) and chair of the President's Science Advisory Committee, convened a group of experts to brainstorm national surveillance strategies for Eisenhower. Killian's panel recommended the use of small scientific satellites. American intelligence officials had known about the potential to launch satellites with rockets as early as 1946, when a report commissioned by the US military (*Preliminary Design of an Experimental World-Circling Spaceship*) stated that a satellite could theoretically be launched into orbit by a rocket. The report called the satellite "one of the most potent scientific tools of the 20th century" and noted that it was "comparable to the explosion of the atomic bomb."

Rather than pilots taking intermittent photographs, the satellite proposed by the panel allowed for continuous and long-term monitoring of the enemy and eliminated the need to risk pilots' lives in airplane surveillance. The panel further advised that Eisenhower begin developing America's first spy satellites. Eisenhower agreed. The project was classified, and not even von Braun, the country's top rocket designer, knew about it.

Before Eisenhower could develop and deploy satellites, he had to overcome a legal obstacle. There were no established laws governing space. Did a country's borders extend vertically into the atmosphere, and if so, how far? If the United States launched a satellite and flew it over an enemy country—the Soviet Union, for example—did that constitute an act of war? Eisenhower needed a way to force the issue of freedom of space without threatening other countries.

The International Council of Scientific Unions coincidentally provided Eisenhower's solution. The organization was preparing to unite the world through science: July 1957 through December 1958 was designated as the International Geophysical Year. Countries were invited to collect and share scientific data about the Earth and launch scientific satellites. The IGY's humanitarian mission provided a nonthreatening (and convenient) reason to launch world-circling satellites and thereby establish the freedom-of-space principle without confrontation. On March 14, 1955, the US announced its plan to launch a satellite as part of the yearlong scientific project. Not to be outdone, two months later the Soviets announced that they would launch a satellite as well.

By that summer, Korolev's expanding rocket program was gaining momentum. His proposal for the R-7 rocket was approved. But the old Kapustin Yar test range could not accommodate the huge intercontinental ballistic missile, capable of carrying a nuclear warhead or a future Soviet satellite. On June 7, the Soviets broke ground on a new launch facility in the desert of Kazakhstan, 1,300 miles from Moscow. When it was finished, it would be the world's first spaceport: the Baikonur Cosmodrome, the site of some of the most historic rocket launches of the twentieth century. As the US and USSR began preparations for the IGY, the stage was set for the first battle of the space race.

The quest for satellites had begun.

STAGE II

The Quest for Satellites

CHAPTER 14

A RED MOON RISES

February 20, 1956, outside Moscow
Korolev's rocket workshop, OKB-1

The secret hangar "stretched upward like a many-meters-tall glass tower-aquarium . . . the windows covered by a thick layer of white paint—protection from curious eyes," recalled Sergei Khrushchev, the son of Soviet leader Nikita Khrushchev. Sergei, an engineer, had joined his father and a group of Soviet officials on a tour of Korolev's rocket workshop, known as OKB-1. The well-lit room had to be large to accommodate the massive rocket before them. "Crowding together at the entrance, we all stared silently at this miracle of technology." The visitors inspected the rocket from every angle. The Soviet leader was humbled by Korolev's creation, saying, "We did everything but lick it to see how it tasted." His official visit was a sign of Korolev's increasing influence and, Korolev hoped, an indication that Khruschev would authorize the R-7 to launch a satellite.

Korolev explained that a missile needed a range of approximately 5,000 miles to reach US targets, and he was confident such a range was eventually possible for the R-7 rocket. A vehicle this powerful rendered contemporary air defense systems useless because it soared high, fast, and well out of enemy target range. Calculations had shown that five nuclear weapons would be enough to destroy England; a few more would lay waste to France.

"Yes, a terrible force," said Khrushchev. "The last war was bloody, but with such warheads, it has become simply unthinkable; five warheads and a whole country gone. Terrible."

"I would like you to know about still another project," said Korolev. Sensing the momentum he had gained, he led the group to a nearby stand that supported a metallic sphere model with rods protruding on all sides. His visitors were confused. Compared to what they had seen thus far, the metal orb was unremarkable.

It was a satellite, Korolev explained. With Khrushchev's support, he was certain his team could use the R-7 missile to launch the satellite into orbit around the Earth like an artificial moon. A similar satellite could one day be fitted with a camera, able to observe the planet from space, photographing anything the Soviet government might want to see—and things other world governments preferred to keep secret. The satellite project would not detract from ongoing defense work, and he pointed out that it carried immense propaganda value as well. The Americans were already working on a satellite, he cautioned. If the USSR could launch one before the US, it would be the first country on Earth to put a man-made object into space. The superiority of Soviet technology would be undeniable. Korolev assured Khrushchev that he could easily replace the R-7's warhead with the satellite and launch it.

Khrushchev listened attentively to the chief designer. He examined the satellite model closely; Korolev's proposal was sound. Based on what Khrushchev had seen already, Korolev was a capable and visionary engineer. His team's inventions were brilliant, and the workshop was equally impressive.

"The main priority is security for the country," Khrushchev reminded Korolev. But as long as the satellite did not interfere with other defense projects, why not attempt to beat the Americans to space?

With Khrushchev's final approval, Korolev's design bureau was cleared to launch the Soviet Union's first satellite.

CHAPTER 15

ARMY VS. NAVY

While Korolev was receiving approval to launch his Earth satellite in the USSR, von Braun's Huntsville team, operating under the US Army, was in a heated competition with the US Navy for the privilege of launching America's first satellite. These were the pre-NASA days, when every rocket and satellite project was a military operation and, therefore, highly classified. The only information available to the American public was that their country was attempting to launch a satellite in celebration of the International Geophysical Year.

Von Braun desperately wanted his Army Ballistic Missile Agency (ABMA) team to be chosen for the assignment. This was what they had come to the United States to do, and a satellite was the next step in space exploration. The army detailed their plans to partner with the Jet Propulsion Laboratory (JPL) in Pasadena, California, for the IGY satellite launch. Von Braun's group would provide a modified

Redstone rocket called Jupiter-C (a beefed-up version of the V-2) as a launch vehicle. The multistage rocket had a detachable nose cone that could be easily adapted to accommodate a simple five-pound satellite for release into Earth's orbit. To build the scientific satellite, the JPL team, headed by William Pickering, partnered with a University of Iowa geophysicist, James Van Allen.

Van Allen hypothesized that a band of radiation encircled the Earth. Along with a team of graduate students working in the basement of the University of Iowa's physics building, he developed a cosmic ray detector to be carried on board the satellite to test for the existence of radiation bands. If Van Allen's hypothesis was correct, that radiation could be a hazardous obstacle to future spaceflight pioneers.

The competing project was designed by the Naval Research Laboratory (NRL), a research institution within the US Navy, and led by John P. Hagen. Their proposal would use the navy's multistage Vanguard rocket to launch a satellite that would gather data about the shape of the Earth and measure fluctuations in its gravitational field. Von Braun's modified "Old Reliable" Redstone was ready to go, but the Vanguard rocket was still under development, its third stage not yet completed.

From the beginning, von Braun was skeptical that the navy could have their rocket ready in time. He was confident in his team's hardware and that their proposal would win the satellite project. When the navy's proposal was chosen, von Braun's team was shocked and angry. "We had worked hard in the short time we had to put it together," engineer Randy Clinton recalled. Clinton was one of many Americans who worked with the Germans at the Redstone Arsenal. They were proud of the job they were doing and admired von Braun's leadership. But the Germans wondered if it was politics, not pursuit of the best proposal, that had cost them the job. The Redstone rocket was based on the V-2 design, a missile with a lethal reputation. Because the decision had been made behind closed doors, it was impossible to know for sure.

The truth was, however, that the navy had a superior scientific proposal and satellite, and their rocket was highly efficient—or would be once it was finished. The Vanguard may have been unproven, but it was also a 100 percent *American* design. Von Braun didn't care how impressive the navy's rocket and satellite looked on paper. He was certain it would fail.

Von Braun worried that delays caused by the underdeveloped Vanguard rocket increased the chances of the Russians beating America to space. He resolved to be ready when the time came. He would not defy direct orders and launch the army satellite, but he wouldn't follow those orders to the letter, either. If he had played by the rules at the end of the war, he might not have made it out of Germany alive. So von Braun and Dr. William Pickering of the Jet Propulsion Laboratory hatched a plan.

The two men agreed to continue developing their satellite in secret. The army was technically forbidden to work on its satellite because the navy had won the right to launch first, but no one said anything about members of von Braun's team continuing the satellite work on their own time. Peenemünde veteran Ernst Stuhlinger carried out calculations for the project in his home garage. Once, when Randy Clinton heard an inspection team was on its way from Washington, he stashed the satellite in the trunk of his car to hide it from them.

On September 20, 1956, at Cape Canaveral, Florida, the Huntsville engineers conducted a scheduled test of the Jupiter-C rocket, the same rocket included in their satellite proposal. The test had been approved, but the Pentagon had concerns about the rocket's fourth stage—its satellite compartment. Military brass in Washington feared von Braun would secretly launch the satellite before the navy team had completed their work, stealing Vanguard's thunder. Just before the launch, von Braun received a phone call from his superior, Major General Bruce Medaris. "Wernher, I must put you under direct orders personally to inspect that fourth stage to make sure it is not live," he said. By "live," Medaris meant carrying a satellite. Von Braun had no intention of launching a satellite that day, but he managed to make it into the history books anyway. The Jupiter-C set a record for an American rocket, soaring to an altitude of six hundred miles and traveling a distance of more than thirty-three hundred miles. Von Braun was overjoyed by the record-setting flight, dancing when he heard the news. If the rocket had been carrying a satellite instead of a nose cone stuffed with sand, America could have achieved another record that day: launching the world's first satellite.

News of the Jupiter-C's successful flight was not formally announced, but the information leaked days later. Wildly exaggerated details of the event reached the Soviet Union, and an alarmed Korolev mistakenly believed von Braun had attempted a satellite launch. Were the Americans that close to succeeding? The misinformation heightened tensions for Korolev as he raced to save his struggling satellite project, known as Object D, which was mired in technical problems—big ones.

CHAPTER 16

OBJECT D

Object D tipped the scales at a hefty 1.3 tons. The R-7 could not lift it off the ground. In mid-November 1956, Mikhail Tikhonravov, who helped Korolev design it, had an idea. "What if we make the satellite a little lighter, a little simpler," he proposed. Why did the satellite need to contain so many scientific instruments if their main goal was to achieve orbit? Korolev agreed. The simplified satellite would house only one or two radio transmitters and a power source. Tikhonravov's solution also slashed production time and costs. The new, streamlined satellite could be fully redesigned and tested in a couple of months. If it was destroyed during launch, assembling a replacement would be fast and affordable.

As the weeks passed, pressure increased for members of Korolev's team working on the new, smaller satellite. Viacheslav Lappo, among the youngest of the engineers, was tasked with the development of a transmitter to broadcast audio signals back to Earth from Object D. But Lappo faced a difficult truth. He had no method by which to guarantee the signal's clarity in space. Temperature fluctuations, cosmic radiation, even meteorites could disrupt the transmission. It was impossible to predict and control the variables that determined success or failure.

Lappo was at his desk late one night when the work-obsessed chief designer dropped in to check on his progress. Korolev didn't sleep much, despite his grueling schedule. He asked Lappo to play the signal for him. The steady *bleep-bleep-bleep* sound delighted Korolev, who asked, "Couldn't you make it squeak a word of some kind?"

While Korolev finalized his satellite and prepared to launch it with his R-7, in the US, von Braun grew increasingly concerned that the Soviets would succeed first. Convinced that the navy could not build and perfect Vanguard's top stage in time, he devised another secret backup plan. A Jupiter-C rocket was moved into what he called a "long-term storage test." To military leaders at the Pentagon, it looked as if the team was conducting a routine experiment. In reality, von Braun was safely storing a rocket that could launch a satellite on short notice.

As more time passed, intelligence reports confirmed von Braun's worst fear, that the Soviets could soon launch their satellite. The Vanguard still wasn't ready. In his desperation to beat the Soviets, von Braun made one final offer, suggesting that the navy's satellite be launched into orbit with the army's Jupiter-C rocket, instead of Vanguard.

The navy declined the deal. Exasperated, von Braun had a few choice words for John Hagen, director of the Vanguard program. "Tell him if he wants to, he can paint 'Vanguard' right up the side of my rocket. He can do anything he wants to, but he is to use my rocket, not his, because my rocket will work and his won't."

It was a last-ditch play and it had failed. Like it or not, the navy would attempt to launch the first American satellite, and von Braun would be forced to watch from the sidelines along with the rest of the country. He believed that his chance would come eventually. He just hoped that moment arrived before a Soviet satellite.

CHAPTER 17

SPUTNIK

The weather was unseasonably warm for autumn in the desert of Kazakhstan. It was launch day at the Baikonur Cosmodrome. The new rocket complex had been completed in just two years.

Korolev's newly redesigned satellite was packed into the nose cone of the nine-story R-7 rocket. Object D had shrunk. Now the satellite was about the size of a basketball, weighing just under 184 pounds. It gleamed like polished silver, per Korolev's instructions that it be light-reflective to increase its chances of visibility to the naked eye. He wanted anyone, whether they owned a telescope or not, to be able to see what the Soviets had achieved. Four antennae attached to the sphere would be triggered after it was ejected into orbit. The satellite had been renamed Sputnik, Russian for "fellow traveler."

Fifteen minutes before launch, the area surrounding the pad was cleared of all personnel. At the ten-minute mark, Korolev arrived in the command crew's bunker to observe liftoff. He was visibly on edge. He reacted to the slightest sound or comment, "instantly on the alert to see what was going on," one witness recalled.

"Ten minutes to readiness," a voice boomed through the loudspeaker. Twenty-four-year-old lieutenant Boris Chekunov was responsible for activating the launch. He placed his hand on the launch key and waited.

"Kliuch na start!" announced an operator.

Chekunov turned the key on his panel from left to right.

"Pusk!" Chekunov pushed the launch button. All five of Valentin Glushko's powerful engines exploded to life. Vibrations shook the bunker as the 273-ton rocket thundered on the launchpad.

"Est' kontakt pod'ema!" At this final "Contact liftoff" command, the support arms of the launch complex attached to the rocket fell open. In a moment of world-defining firsts, the R-7 was on its own. From the world's first spaceport, the first intercontinental ballistic missile soared from the sand of the Kazakhstan desert toward a sea of black sky. If Korolev succeeded, it would punch the world's first satellite into orbit.

Inside the bunker it was too soon to celebrate. The stoic chief designer was unmoved. Once the rocket was out of visual range, time seemed to stop. "There was absolute silence," one Soviet official recalled. "All that could be heard was the breathing of the people and the quiet static in the loudspeaker. . . . And then, from very far off, there appeared, at first very quietly, and then louder and louder, those '*bleep-bleeps*' that confirmed it was in orbit." Everything was functioning perfectly—for the moment.

Outside, Viacheslav Lappo and his colleague Konstantin Gringauz sat inside a van, headphones over their ears, straining to hear Sputnik's signal. When the first bleeps sounded, they immediately called Korolev to report.

Korolev continued to hold his emotions in check. He would relax when the signal returned after Sputnik's first orbit was completed and not a moment before. The chief designer and a number of his crew left the bunker and made their way to Lappo and Gringauz's van to wait for Sputnik's next transmission.

An hour and a half later, Lappo heard Sputnik's steady beat return and shouted, "It's there! It's there! Turn on the tape recorders!" As the sun rose, Korolev finally rejoiced with his team, who laughed and kissed one another on each cheek. When their "fellow traveler" once again broadcast its reliable signal, the teary-eyed men looked to the sky and listened as Sputnik called back to them from the stars.

Korolev addressed the team around him. He spoke of the enormity of their accomplishment, congratulating all of them, taking care to acknowledge "the junior specialists, technicians, and designers," thanking them for their "titanic labor." As Lappo's transmitter broadcast its repetitive bleeps from inside Sputnik, amateur radio operators around the world began to hear the first-ever man-made sound to be transmitted from outer space.

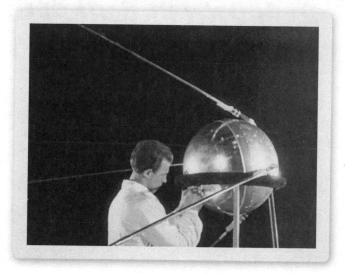

The world's first satellite, Sputnik I.

CHAPTER 18

BLEEP-BLEEP-BLEEP

OCTOBER 4, 1957

As Sputnik zoomed around the Earth, von Braun was on his way to a cocktail party at the Redstone Arsenal officers' club, unaware that the Soviets had successfully launched a satellite. He and his boss at ABMA, Major General Bruce Medaris, had spent the day escorting President Eisenhower's nominee for defense secretary, Neil McElroy, around their facilities. Von Braun stopped by his office before the party, and the telephone rang.

"What do you think of it?" a British newspaper reporter asked.

"Think of what?" asked von Braun.

"The Russian satellite. The one they just orbited."

Von Braun arrived at the party and immediately relayed the information to McElroy. "We knew they were going to do it!" he said. "Vanguard will never make it. We have the hardware on the shelf. For God's sake, turn us loose and let us do something. We can put that satellite up in sixty days, Mr. McElroy! Just give us the green light and sixty days."

Medaris did a quick mental calculation of the time required to move their Jupiter-C rocket from its "long-term storage test" and make the satellite operational. He knew there was no way they could do it within the two months von Braun was promising. He had to rein in the headstrong engineer. "Ninety days," Medaris said to von Braun, who immediately understood. He backed off and agreed to the additional month. Without a promise from McElroy, or permission from his superiors, Medaris secretly told von Braun to "get the stuff out on the floor and go to work on it just as if we had a directive to proceed."

As a new day dawned on October 5, fourteen-year-old Homer Hickam Jr.—who later became a NASA engineer—was sound asleep in his cozy bed when his mother awakened him. She looked worried. "Come listen," she said. Hickam dressed and made his way downstairs. While he ate buttered toast and sipped hot chocolate, his mother turned on the radio. He expected to hear rock and roll music. Instead, he heard a *bleep-bleep-bleep* sound coming from the radio and the announcer's voice saying that "the tone was coming from something called Sputnik. It was Russian and it was in space." Hickam's mother knew that science-fiction novels and magazines fascinated her smart and curious son. In their small coal-mining town of Coalwood, West Virginia, he was like many American kids who were swept up in the science-fiction craze of the 1950s. Hickam's mother hoped her son could explain the strange sound. "What is this thing, Sonny?" she asked.

Hickam knew exactly what it was and why it mattered. Someone had finally done it! While he slept, the Soviets had launched the world's first Earth-orbiting satellite and delivered a punishing technological blow to America. The man-made moon orbited the planet every ninety-eight minutes, broadcasting its telltale *bleep-bleep-bleep* from space.

That evening, in the backyard of his family's home, Hickam waited for Sputnik to appear in the night sky. He spotted it just as Korolev had intended, without the aid of a telescope. "The bright little ball [moved] majestically across the narrow star field between the ridgelines," Hickam later wrote. "I stared at it with no less rapt attention than if it had been God Himself in a golden chariot riding overhead. It soared with what seemed to me inexorable and dangerous purpose, as if there were no power in the universe that could stop it." Inspired by Sputnik's appearance over Coalwood, Hickam started his own rocket club with a group of his friends, the Big Creek Missile Agency.

There was no stopping what Sputnik had started. It was the dawn of the space age, and all around the world, Korolev's satellite was sparking the imaginations of young people like Hickam, who had only read of such things in science-fiction novels. They watched

Sputnik succeed and believed that they could also be a part of it. The dream of spaceflight had become reality.

Not everyone was inspired by Sputnik's arrival. Some people hardly noticed or cared. Still others were frightened, as newspapers thudded onto doorsteps with ominous headlines: "Russians Win Race to Launch Earth Satellite," "Space Age Is Here," "Russia Wins Race into Outer Space," "Russians Launch First Artificial Moon." People across the country crowded around radios and televisions to listen for its signal. When night fell, they looked up, scanning the sky for the mysterious silver ball racing around the planet. Imaginations ran wild with doomsday scenarios. Was the satellite carrying a bomb? What did the bleeping sound mean? Was it a code of some sort? Did Sputnik have cameras aboard that could take pictures of classified American military bases? And the most frightening prospect of all: Was a missile powerful enough to launch a satellite into orbit also capable of launching a nuclear weapon against the United States?

At a press conference five days after the historic appearance of Sputnik, Eisenhower tried to ease the country's fears by downplaying its significance, saying that Sputnik didn't "raise [his] apprehensions, not one iota." It wasn't what some Americans wanted to hear. How could their president remain calm in the face of this disturbing turn of events? Didn't he care about the loss of American prestige? They worried that he was underestimating the threat and was dangerously out of touch.

Eisenhower was not out of touch. Far from it. The Central Intelligence Agency (CIA) had previously warned him that a Soviet satellite launch was possible. In fact, Eisenhower was *relieved* that the Soviets had been the first to launch a satellite, because they had unwittingly established the freedom of space principle. Now any nation launching a satellite that flew over a foreign country could expect to do so without provoking hostility. Sputnik had proven to be a windfall for American national security interests. Eisenhower would be able to deploy secret spy satellites to monitor the Soviet Union, which he believed was more important than any scientific gain. What Eisenhower failed to understand was the demoralizing impact Sputnik would have on his country.

The appearance of this strange new Soviet technology heightened tensions as the Cold War entered a new phase. The stage was set for a prestige fight between the United States and the Soviet Union. Rather than risk annihilating one another with nuclear weapons, the rivalry would unfold in the race to outer space. At stake would be recognition as the world's dominant scientific power. The Soviet Union had taunted America like a playground bully who had thrown the first punch. But when America tried to hit back, it would be swinging at a ghost.

CHAPTER 19

THE INVISIBLE MAN

Korolev's Sputnik victory made him one of the most important men in the Soviet Union. Intelligence agents feared he could be kidnapped or assassinated. He had to disappear before anyone in the West could discover his true identity.

An invisible man could not be threatened, Soviet officials reasoned, but he couldn't be acknowledged either. Korolev was forbidden to claim public credit for any of his achievements, including Sputnik. Around 1957, his name became a state secret and, along with Valentin Glushko's and those of several other key missile program designers, began disappearing from historical records. If Korolev was mentioned at all, it was only by his title, "chief designer," to conceal his identity from the world.

During this time, the Nobel Prize Committee contacted the Soviet Union requesting the name of the person responsible for Sputnik. Khrushchev refused to disclose Korolev's identity, declaring that the achievement belonged to the Soviet people, not to one person. If Korolev felt any bitterness about not being allowed to claim public credit for his satellite, it did not diminish his desire to innovate. Sputnik, the world would soon discover, was just the beginning.

In the United States, news of the world's first orbiting satellite had been announced in the *New York Times* with a six-column-wide headline, historically used only for declarations of war: "Soviet Fires Earth Satellite into Space; It Is Circling the Globe at 18,000 M.P.H.; Sphere Tracked in 4 Crossings over U.S." By contrast, in the Soviet Union, the press announcement was barely noticeable, buried in the morning edition of the Soviet newspaper, *Pravda*, beneath a larger headline that read: "Winter Is an Urgent Task." Khrushchev had not anticipated the international outcry over Sputnik's launch. Like Eisenhower in the US, his priority was defense, not scientific experiments. But the worldwide media craze in the wake of Sputnik signaled to Khrushchev that Korolev's pet satellite projects could be a propaganda gold mine. By deliberately hiding the Soviets' weaknesses while hyping Korolev's victories in the media, Khrushchev would craft an exaggerated image of the Soviet Union's scientific and military power. It got him thinking: What if Korolev could do it again?

The fortieth anniversary of the Russian Revolution was one month away. Perhaps the Soviet Union could quickly capitalize on

Sputnik's success with a second satellite launch timed to coincide with the occasion? Korolev hesitated. There were consequences to consider. If the next launch failed, the achievement of Sputnik could be diminished. And further developments on the R-7 would have to be halted to complete the new project on time. It was a risk, but Korolev had a lot to gain by keeping Krushchev happy and knew that his team could have a second satellite ready to launch in time for the anniversary. Korolev not only agreed to the launch, he offered to sweeten the deal: What if Sputnik II carried a live passenger?

PROPAGANDA

The use of propaganda persists. Political advertisements are one of the most common places to encounter this type of rhetoric, as opponents seek to rally support and convince people that their beliefs are superior to their rival's. In the age of the internet, lies and half-truths created by political leaders can spread in less time than it takes to update a social media post.

When enough of these lies and deliberate mistruths go unchecked, they solidify into an erroneous record of history, aided by the immediacy of the internet. During the 2016 presidential election, the Russians carried out a massive social media attack against the US designed to compromise the integrity of the election.

CHAPTER 20

LAIKA AND THE COSMO-MUTT COVER-UP

On the afternoon of October 31, 1957, a small, three-year-old female stray dog named Laika was placed inside the Sputnik II satellite with food and water. Outfitted with a special space suit, she was sealed in a cabin of the thirteen-foot, cone-shaped capsule. A separate cabin contained the life-support system, power sources, and other scientific instruments. The weather was cold, and the temperature inside Laika's capsule was controlled to keep the dog comfortable until launch. Later that night, Laika's capsule was placed atop the rocket sitting on the launchpad at the Baikonur Cosmodrome. Korolev and his team were confident they could boost the dog into orbit—but they also knew that they couldn't bring her back. The technology to return a living creature safely to Earth did not yet exist. Laika's voyage would be a one-way trip.

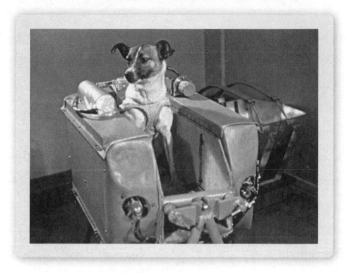

Laika, the Russian street dog turned unwitting space traveler.

Before risking a human life, the Soviets would first use a dog to test their ability to successfully launch living beings into space and learn how their bodies reacted to weightlessness. Homeless dogs were abundant in Moscow. Flight doctors believed these strays would be the most resilient live test subjects, because they had learned to survive on their own.

The affectionate Laika was smart and loved to run and play. She easily adapted to training. Her small size was another asset, because the capsule could not accommodate more than fifteen pounds of cargo. Laika underwent surgery to implant transmitters that would monitor her vital signs and relay her physical condition during the flight. "Everyone was very concerned," recalled Viktor Yazdovsky, the son of the flight doctor who had cared for Laika throughout her training. "They knew she would not return from her journey." His father brought Laika home to spend time with their family because he "wanted to do something nice for her." Perhaps the elder Yazdovsky also wanted to ease his conscience.

On November 3, after sitting inside the capsule for three days while the launch procedures were completed, Laika finally lifted off, becoming the first living creature to orbit the Earth. It was another victory for the Soviets. Korolev had once again managed an extraordinary feat. How long Laika could survive, however, was unknown.

At liftoff, Laika's implanted sensors communicated her vital signs to ground control. Her suffering as a result of the noise and speed at launch was evident in her heart rate, which leaped to three times its normal speed. Once in orbit, the temperature inside her cabin began to rise. Adequate insulation for space capsules had not yet been developed. Soon the dog was suffering temperatures approaching one hundred degrees Fahrenheit.

The initial Soviet news reports proclaimed that Laika had lived nine days. It was a lie designed to minimize negative perceptions of the experiment while emphasizing the accomplishment of launching a living being into space. In truth, the doomed little dog probably survived just a few hours and succumbed to the extreme heat in the capsule after completing three full orbits. These details about how long Laika actually survived were not publicized until 2011, when a letter originating in Soviet-era Russia was declassified. The truth had been hidden for fifty-four years.

What did it mean that the Soviets were willing to sacrifice this animal in an effort to make human spaceflight possible? Was it justified, or was it senseless cruelty? It depended who you asked. It still does. At the time, some Russians believed it was a necessary step in advancing their technology. "The Russians love dogs," a Soviet official protested. "This has been done not for the sake of cruelty but for the benefit of humanity." Oleg Gazenko, the principal investigator responsible for sending Laika into space, later admitted that he regretted her death. Undoubtedly, others were also saddened and believed that the dog's sacrifice was unnecessary. In the United States, the editorial board of the *New York Times* lamented Laika's fate, calling her "the shaggiest, lonesomest, saddest dog in all history." Yet Laika undeniably lives on in books, songs, and untold quantities of Soviet-era memorabilia. The little stray dog that blasted into spaceflight history aboard Korolev's rocket became a Russian cultural icon and symbol of the Soviet space program—not that she ever had a choice in the matter.

CHAPTER 21

THE INVISIBLE WOMAN

The launching of a live dog in a space satellite lit a fire in Washington, DC. President Eisenhower could no longer deny the need for an appropriate American response to the Soviets' space challenge. Von Braun and Van Allen received approval to begin prepping the Jupiter-C rocket and its Explorer 1 satellite for launch. The navy's Vanguard rocket would attempt to launch first, but after that, the army's Redstone Arsenal team would get their chance. Hopefully, between the two rocket teams, one of them would succeed.

In Huntsville, physicist Joyce Neighbors, PhD, was rolling up her sleeves to help von Braun's team do whatever was necessary to make the Explorer 1 launch a success. Neighbors was a team player and one of the few women in the male-dominated technology field of the 1950s. Explorer 1 was the opportunity she had been working toward her entire life. Neighbors played a key role in early American spaceflight, but due to sexism within NASA at the time, her early contribution was deliberately obscured.

Dr. Alice K. (Joyce) Neighbors, photographed in 1976.

When Neighbors was first hired as a mathematician at the Redstone Arsenal, working with von Braun's rocket team, she was elated. Born and raised on a small farm in rural Georgia, Neighbors grew up in a house without running water. But she was smart, she believed in herself, and she was determined to go to college, eventually earning a PhD in physics. Now her dreams of making a difference in the world were coming true.

Future rockets would rely on electronic computers to manage every aspect of the launch sequence and flight. But in the late 1950s, the Jupiter-C's rocket stages fired under manual commands from people. The timing of those commands was calculated by hand. The "computers" were human beings, and Neighbors was one of them. The figures she contributed were indicated on a hand-drawn chart that would be used to plan when to fire the rocket's engines at each stage of the flight.

The lead German engineer, Ernst Stuhlinger, asked everyone involved in the creation of the chart to sign it. In acknowledgment of her contribution, Neighbors was asked to sign her name—but not her *full* name. Stuhlinger did not want anyone to know that one of the signatures belonged to a woman. He feared it would negatively reflect on the document's credibility. Neighbors didn't hesitate. She picked up her pen and signed her initials as Stuhlinger requested. "I had to wear a veneer in those days," she recalled years later. "That is not something that comes naturally to me, but it was an honor to be asked. It was a privilege to be a part of something larger than myself. I also knew I was making a place for all the women who would come after me. Signing that chart was one of the great honors of my life." Today, Dr. Joyce Neighbors's historic contribution to spaceflight is acknowledged in an exhibit at the US Space & Rocket Center (USSRC) museum in Huntsville, Alabama, where her portrait hangs next to the chart bearing her signature.

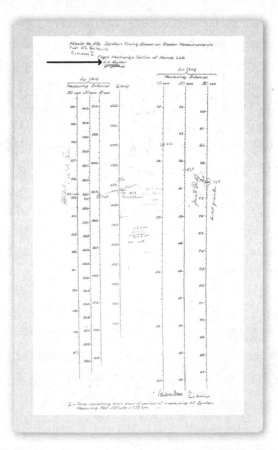

Dr. Neighbors's incomplete signature did not include her full name, to cover up the fact that she was a woman.

Hidden Figures

Another group of female NASA employees overcame both gender and racial discrimination. Their roles were obscured in early histories of the space program because they were Black. During the Jim Crow era, African Americans working for the agency were restricted to segregated work spaces, bathroom facilities, and cafeterias. Katherine Johnson, Dorothy Vaughan, and Mary Jackson worked as "computers," calculating the complex mathematics for the engineers working in the space program and other projects at NASA. While these pioneering women did not work directly with von Braun's group, some of their contributions were crucial to the future of crewed spaceflight with Projects Mercury and Gemini, as well as the Apollo-era missions. In December 2019, all three women were awarded congressional gold medals.

Johnson, in particular, would help narrow the distance between the Soviet Union and the US during the space race. Two days shy of his Earth-orbiting launch aboard *Friendship 7*, John Glenn hesitated. Before he would agree to be blasted into space, he insisted that Johnson double-check the accuracy of his flight's trajectory data. The astronaut didn't trust the numbers generated by NASA's IBM electronic computer. He trusted Johnson.

"If she says they're good, then I'm ready to go," he said. In 2015, at the age of ninety-seven, Johnson accepted the Presidential Medal of Freedom from President Barack Obama, who cited her as a pioneering example of African American women in science, technology, engineering, and mathematics (STEM).

At the age of ten, future NASA mathematician Katherine Johnson entered high school, and by age eighteen, she had earned dual degrees in math and French from West Virginia State College. She retired from the agency in 1986, after thirty-three years of groundbreaking work in spaceflight.

CHAPTER 22

THE AMERICAN SATELLITE

In early December 1957, the US Navy's seventy-two-foot, three-stage Vanguard rocket sat on a launchpad at Cape Canaveral, Florida, with a satellite nestled in its nose cone. With their two successful Sputnik launches, the Soviets were ahead in the Cold War battle for scientific supremacy. It was time to strike back. Millions of people around the world tuned in to watch the historic flight on television.

Liftoff was "a thing of beauty," reported California's *Humboldt Standard* newspaper. The rocket rose, and for the first few moments, the launch appeared to be going as planned. Then four short feet from the pad, it collapsed and exploded into "a tremendous orange ball of flame . . . followed by an awesome black cloud of smoke." The rocket was a complete failure, but the satellite was safely ejected from the inferno. It landed nearby and began broadcasting its audio signal as if it were in orbit, like a baby bird that had tumbled from the nest too soon. The headlines describing the failed attempt reflected

America's disappointment and indignation. "Sputter, Sputter, Fizzle, Fizzle, Plop!!" wailed the *Humboldt Standard*'s headline. "US Fires Dudnik."

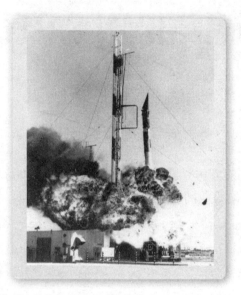

The Navy's Vanguard rocket explodes on the launchpad.

In the Soviet Union, *Pravda* published a reproduction of the front page of London's *Daily Herald*. The article included two images: one of Vanguard before liftoff, and next to it, an image of the resulting explosion. The headline read: "Oh, What a Flopnik!"[5] Above this was a single line: *Reklama i Deistvitelnost*, which meant "Publicity

---

5 The Vanguard program eventually achieved success on March 17, 1958, by placing the world's first solar-powered satellite into orbit. Although contact with it was lost in 1964, Vanguard 1 remains the oldest artificial satellite in Earth orbit.

and Reality." The government was pointing out to *Pravda* readers that while America made promises about its technology, in reality, they could not compete with the mighty Soviet Union.

"Goldstone Has the Bird!"

The following month, at Cape Canaveral, Florida, US Army major general Bruce Medaris was determined to help Wernher von Braun prove that the Soviet Union wasn't the only country capable of launching a satellite. With the Vanguard failure, all eyes turned to von Braun's team.

The army had a three-day window in which to launch Explorer 1. After that, the navy would get a chance to make up for its humiliating failure with a second Vanguard launch.

Von Braun, Pickering, and Van Allen had been ordered to Washington, DC, to hold a press conference once the satellite was in orbit. Medaris and von Braun's longtime crew chief, Kurt Debus, would oversee operations at the cape. Debus was one of von Braun's most trusted engineers. The two had worked together since the Peenemünde days. Back then, the army investigators had classified Debus as an "ardent Nazi" who had denounced his colleagues to the Gestapo. Debus's file was classified along with those of others who had been part of Operation Paperclip, and he was allowed to enter the United States anyway.[6]

On the morning of January 29, Medaris and Debus realized

---

6 Kurt Debus went on to serve as the first director of NASA's John F. Kennedy Space Center. During World War II, he was a member of the Nazi SS.

that the jet stream was going to be a problem. The wave of air that circulates constantly over the United States at varying altitudes was moving at an unusually high speed. It could tear the rocket apart. When conditions failed to improve, the launch was rescheduled for the next day. But the jet stream surged stronger and the launch was canceled for a second time.

Around seven a.m. on the third day, the team finally heard some hopeful news. The jet stream had relented. Things looked good.

They were *go* for launch.

By ten p.m., the countdown had begun. Engineers and other technicians crowded into a Quonset hut a few miles from the launchpad. The air inside, Medaris said, "seemed charged with electricity." At 10:48 p.m., the launch commenced. "As the missile started its slow, majestic rise, almost every voice" joined in a chorus "that sounded like a prayer, saying, 'Go, baby, go!'" It rose "up and up. Faster and faster." Data from the rocket streamed to the ground control station. Engineers watched for any indication that something was wrong during the four hundred seconds that had elapsed since launch. In that time, Ernst Stuhlinger had been waiting in a nearby hangar. Aided by the chart signed by himself, Joyce Neighbors, and others, Stuhlinger jammed his finger onto the red button that fired the rocket's second stage. Then came the hard part: waiting.

Early reports were good. One of the first tracking stations, in

Antigua, locked onto the satellite's signal, but it was still too soon to declare victory. Only a confirmation of the satellite's signal at the Earthquake Valley tracking station in California meant that orbit had been achieved. Forty minutes later, Medaris received a wire message from the secretary of the army, Wilber Brucker, in Washington:

I'm out of coffee and we are running low on cigarettes. What do I do now?

Send out for more and sweat it out with the rest of us, Medaris replied.

Soon after, technicians were able to verify that all four stages had fired successfully. The team had done all they could. The flight appeared stable from the ground, but until the Explorer 1 signal pinged the Goldstone Tracking Station in California, no one knew for sure.

Around midnight, someone handed Medaris a piece of paper with the words *Goldstone has the bird!* It was confirmation of the satellite's signal. Explorer 1 had achieved a wider orbit than anticipated, which explained the delay. "I repeated the words on the paper out loud," Medaris later wrote. People cheered. From a nearby loudspeaker, the familiar voice of President Eisenhower announced that the United States had successfully launched an Earth satellite.

At one thirty a.m., von Braun, Pickering, and Van Allen held a press conference at the National Academy of Sciences in Washington, DC.

"We have firmly established our foothold in space," von Braun told reporters. "We will never give it up again." The three men held an Explorer 1 model overhead as cameras flashed.

Left to right: Dr. William Pickering, Dr. James Van Allen, and Wernher von Braun triumphantly hoist a model of Explorer I overhead at the press conference on February 1, 1958.

Not only had America launched its first satellite, but it had also snatched an important victory from the Soviets. Explorer 1 carried equipment that allowed Van Allen to make the first scientific discovery in outer space. His cosmic ray detector proved his hypothesis that the radioactive band existed. Now known as the Van Allen belt, the "two donuts of seething radiation" held in place by the planet's magnetic field help shield Earth from the sun's deadly cosmic rays.

In the Soviet Union, Korolev felt the pressure of von Braun's triumph. The designer's desk was covered with English-language newspapers boasting about the victorious American response to Sputnik. At his side, a translator worked throughout the night, transcribing the details of the American victory, as the determined Korolev contemplated his next move.

STAGE III

The Quest for the Moon

CHAPTER 23

NASA IS BORN

The United States had finally answered the Soviets' satellite challenge, but for the time being, its rival was more advanced and better organized. Von Braun spoke candidly to reporters, both in print and over the airwaves, about how far America still needed to go to beat the USSR. He was constantly trying to drum up support for his work. Given how closely Korolev followed American media from inside the Soviet Union, he likely saw, heard, and read many of von Braun's public statements about the status of the American program, as well as his thoughts on Soviet accomplishments.

"Their recent progress is phenomenal and the momentum of Soviet science is formidable," von Braun wrote in an August 1958 article. "We must expect many more Soviet 'firsts' in the field of space rocketry before we can meet their challenge." Soviet ICBMs had carried not one but two satellites into orbit. Eisenhower knew that America was going to need smart, educated, creative people to compete with the USSR in this rapidly evolving field of science. In September of that year, he signed the National Defense Education Act into law, which set aside federal funds to emphasize the importance of math and science courses in public schools.

Legislation was an important first step, but there was a more urgent organizational problem to be solved. If the US intended to win the space race and cement its position as the most scientifically powerful country in the world, a single entity devoted to the peaceful scientific pursuit of spaceflight was essential.

Since 1915, NACA (the National Advisory Committee for Aeronautics) had been the organization devoted to the study and advancement of the science of flight. Simple enough if the aircraft were the types of planes flown by early NACA member Orville Wright. But a lot had changed in the forty-three years since the Wright brothers skipped off the sand and into the skies above Kitty Hawk, North Carolina, taking flight for the first time. On July 29, 1958, President Eisenhower signed the National Aeronautics and Space Act. NACA was replaced by a new civilian agency: the National Aeronautics and Space Administration (NASA).

Vostok and Project Mercury

Since the dawn of time, humankind's dream of traveling to the stars had been a fantasy. Now the chains of gravity had been broken. Human beings were figuring out how to explore the cosmos, with Korolev and von Braun to lead the way. The mysterious chief designer had pulled off an impressive series of surprises, and von Braun expected more Soviet launches with their big R-7 rocket. The next phase for both countries would be their greatest challenge: manned spaceflight. If Korolev and von Braun hoped to realize their lifelong obsession of landing people on the moon, they first had to figure out how to get human beings to and from space safely. Both sides were developing new rockets and life-supporting space capsules. The Soviet program was called Vostok. In America, it was named Project Mercury.

CHAPTER 24

"THE RIGHT STUFF"

Project Mercury was NASA's first spaceflight mission. Its ambitious goals sounded simple when stated in the agency's short, declarative lingo: "Place a manned spacecraft in orbital flight around the Earth. Investigate man's performance capabilities and his ability to function in the environment of space. Recover the man and the spacecraft safely." But the description understated the danger involved. The agency needed people willing to be strapped into a capsule on top of von Braun's fully fueled missile and launched into space. There was no way to know if the rocket would soar or incinerate them when the agonizing countdown finally reached "zero."

Military test pilots made ideal astronaut candidates. They were daredevils by trade, the way some people were schoolteachers or stockbrokers. The highly skilled pilots flew experimental prototypes to the edges of their mechanical capability, gathering data as they tore through the skies at terrifying speeds and breathtaking altitudes. Journalist Tom Wolfe called this rare quality "the right stuff." It was the ability, Wolfe wrote, "to go up in a hurtling piece of machinery" and "pull it back in the last yawning moment—and then go up again *the next day* and the next day, and every next day, even if the series should prove infinite."

On a good day, test pilots didn't crash their planes or die. But the unspoken reality of a test pilot's life was that their job could be deadly. When a pilot took a seat in the cockpit of an untested airplane, he knew he might not survive. The pilots didn't like to talk about it. What was the point? They were never going to be satisfied sitting behind a desk anyway, and NASA wasn't exactly looking for office personnel. The new space agency needed astronauts. To find them, they scoured the country, recruiting skilled, college-educated aviators who had distinguished themselves as test pilots. From a total of 508 service names, the list was whittled down to seven: John Glenn Jr. (US Marine Corps); Walter "Wally" Schirra Jr., Alan Shepard, and Scott Carpenter (US Navy); and Gordon "Gordo" Cooper, Virgil "Gus" Grissom, and Donald "Deke" Slayton (US Air Force). Their service records read like a who's who of American heroes. They flew risky missions in war zones, wore medals, logged thousands of hours in the cockpit, and had built reputations as the best of the best among the elite test-pilot ranks. They would be the first astronauts in America's crewed spaceflight program, Project Mercury, and were known as the Mercury Seven.

Becoming an astronaut tested the limits of each Mercury Seven astronaut's endurance. They studied advanced math and physics and suffered through an extensive battery of invasive psychological and physical examinations. Each test was designed to simulate conditions and situations they might encounter during spaceflight. Some of the more excruciating exams involved needles. Others were downright weird.

"We were treated like a bunch of lab rats," Mercury Seven astronaut Gordo Cooper remembered. "The doctors got real creative, coming up with some unusual tests." One involved inserting a water hose in the ear of a blindfolded astronaut and then pumping cold water into their ear canal. "Just when you thought your eyeballs were going to float away, they would take out the hose and remove the blindfold and jot down some notes on a pad," Cooper wrote. When he asked what the test was for, Cooper was told he didn't need to know. "We were probed, poked, sampled, tested, and in general completely humiliated on a regular basis for the better part of a week."

On April 9, 1959, the Mercury Seven reported to the ballroom of the historic Dolley Madison House in Washington, DC, which thrummed with the voices of eager journalists. Reporters and photographers battled for the best angle to capture the historic scene as America's first astronauts entered the conference room. Cameras and notebooks were temporarily forgotten as the crowd applauded and cheered. With close shaves, short hair, dark suits, and neatly pressed button-down shirts, they were portraits of professionalism, military precision, and dignity. It wasn't enough that the astronauts were qualified pilots. NASA needed them to look the part in order to inspire confidence in the new space program.

Dr. Keith Glennan, NASA's first administrator, stepped to the podium. "These men, the nation's Project Mercury astronauts, are here after a long and perhaps unprecedented series of evaluations which told our medical consultants and scientists of their superb adaptability to their coming flight." The astronauts answered questions about everything from their training and professional backgrounds to how their wives and children felt about their work.

Finally, a reporter fired off the question every American wanted answered: "Could I ask for a show of hands," he asked, "of how many are confident they will come back from outer space?" There was a brief pause. The astronauts glanced around at one another. Then every single hand shot into the air. The room erupted into camera flashes and another round of thunderous applause.

The next week, *Time* magazine declared: "Rarely were history's explorers and discoverers so clearly marked in advance as men of destiny."

All the Mercury Seven astronauts raise their hands when asked who among them expected to return safely from space.

"The Steel Balloon"

MAY 18, 1959

CAPE CANAVERAL, FLORIDA

The rocket NASA planned to use for the Project Mercury missions was America's first ICBM, the Atlas. The air force had first conceived of the rocket in early 1946. Nine days after the Mercury Seven were introduced to the world, John Glenn and his fellow astronauts observed the Atlas in a test launch at the cape. Glenn recalled the mid-May evening when they gathered about half a mile from the launch complex to observe the test.

"The sight of the Atlas on the launchpad was dramatic enough to have been designed by Disney," he wrote in his memoir. "Searchlights played on the silver rocket, and clouds of water vapor came off it." The rocket appeared solid, he remembered, but it was actually "thin-skinned, basically a steel balloon." At liftoff, "we watched it gain speed, a brilliant phoenix rising into the night sky." When the rocket exploded just one minute after liftoff, the blast "looked like a hydrogen bomb." The astronauts instinctively ducked before remembering they were a safe distance away. Only Alan Shepard spoke. "Well, I'm glad they got that out of the way."

CHAPTER 25

SQUIRREL AND LITTLE ARROW

In the USSR, Korolev moved ahead with his own plans for a future crewed space vehicle. The Vostok capsule was equipped with a life-support system, and for the first time, it would be possible to return passengers safely to Earth. Before Vostok could be approved for testing with a cosmonaut, however, Soviet engineers would risk the lives of more Soviet dogs like Laika.

Korolev's busy schedule did not leave time for the simple comforts of life. He was stern and his temper flared when people fell short of his expectations. However, he seemed to like dogs, visiting the kennels before launches.

Belka ("Squirrel") and Strelka ("Little Arrow") were the dogs selected to test the Vostok. They lifted off on August 19, 1960, from the Baikonur Cosmodrome. While it's impossible to know precisely

Russian space dogs Belka and Strelka.

what the dogs endured, flight data from their body sensors proved that the animals suffered as Laika had before them. Two onboard cameras showed both dogs barely moving during the first part of the flight. Without the sensors, it would have been reasonable for engineers inside Soviet ground control to assume they were dead. Soviet scientists worried that the dogs were proving that the human body could not endure weightlessness. Later on, however, the dogs became more animated, suffering convulsions. During the fourth orbit, the struggling Belka vomited. The sad sight prompted a flight doctor to recommend limiting the flight of a human pilot to a single orbit.

Despite their ordeal, the dogs survived eighteen orbits, spending one day and two hours in space. After a safe landing, Belka and Strelka were declared healthy in a postflight examination. Months later, Strelka gave birth to a litter of puppies, and Khrushchev seized the opportunity to gloat about the health of his country's canine cosmonauts and their mission.

President Kennedy's young daughter, Caroline, received one of Strelka's puppies, named Pushinka ("Fluffy"), as a gift from Khrushchev. Kennedy responded with a polite thank-you note expressing gratitude for remembering his daughter and wrote that the dog's flight from the Soviet Union "was not as dramatic as the flight of her mother, nevertheless, it was a long voyage and she stood it well."

With the successful launch of Vostok and the safe recovery of Belka and Strelka, the Soviets claimed another victory in the space race. They had proven that it was possible to safely return living creatures to Earth with their spacecraft and had taken the lead in the space race. As both countries proceeded with their plans for a human launch, it remained to be seen whether the first person in space would be an American or a Russian.

That question would be answered in the 1960s.

CHAPTER 26

GROWING PAINS AT NASA

In September 1960, von Braun and his group at the Redstone Arsenal were swept up in the tide of NASA's rapid expansion. His team became part of the new civilian space agency. The Redstone Arsenal was renamed the Marshall Space Flight Center (MSFC), and von Braun was appointed its director. For the first time in his life, the engineer was not working for the military. At last, he could devote all his energy to spaceflight.

NASA was growing, but its early Mercury program struggled to keep pace. The air force's unpredictable Atlas rocket had exploded during mutliple test launches. NASA needed a rocket that could be trusted, and pivoted to a less powerful but tried-and-true rocket, von Braun's "Old Reliable" Redstone. The Redstone wasn't powerful enough to achieve the speed and altitude necessary to carry a Mercury space capsule into orbit. Instead of following a flight path around the Earth, the first Mercury mission would be suborbital—flying up and back down in a simple arc. To make it flight ready for an astronout, however, the Redstone required an astounding eight hundred modifications.

These obstacles, and those that would inevitably follow in the race to space, could be overcome with enough money. In November, von Braun had reason to hope when America elected John F. Kennedy as president of the United States. The progressive forty-three-year-old vowed to "get the nation moving again," during a time in which it was mired in the Cold War against the USSR. Von Braun was optimistic that Kennedy would "get the nation moving" toward the moon by allocating lots and lots of money to NASA.

The Four-Inch Flight

On November 21, 1960, thousands of onlookers streamed onto Cocoa Beach in Florida, near Cape Canaveral, to witness the testing of the rocket that was scheduled to eventually carry the first American into space. The modified Redstone was several miles away from spectators but visible on the launch stand in the distance. News crews staged cameras on top of vans and pointed their lenses toward the cape.

In these early days of the space program, basic procedures for launching a rocket were still being developed. At NASA, everyone from the administrators to the engineers and the astronauts was still learning everything they needed to know about how to safely launch, orbit, and land spacecraft. "We were inventing it all as we went along," NASA ground control veteran Gene Kranz wrote in his memoir. Without astronauts aboard, there was no risk to human life. Instead, Redstone's first test would be a public trial by fire for NASA after hundreds of painstaking modifications to von Braun's rocket.

Kranz had been on the job for a little more than a month when he took his seat at the console as a procedures officer that day. As the countdown began, there was "a change in the intensity of the atmosphere in the control room," he wrote. Seconds ticked by. Cameras situated at the launchpad were trained on the rocket, ready to record every moment of the flight. "Precisely at zero on the clock, there was a great cloud of smoke. . . . For a few seconds, there was nothing on the screen in the control room but a smoky sky." It looked as if the rocket had launched so fast that it had already flown out of camera range, but as the control team stared at the smoke-filled image on their monitors, Mercury Redstone came into view.

In a humiliating moment reminiscent of the navy's first Vanguard failure, the Redstone had only risen four inches from the platform before resettling quietly back into place. The failed rocket's saving grace was that it had not exploded on the launchpad.

CHAPTER 27

BLAST RADIUS

There is a reason ground control centers are constructed miles away from launchpads. Any rocket, whether it's carrying a nuclear warhead or a space capsule, can be a weapon of mass destruction if it misfires on the ground. Rockets are filled with highly combustible fuel and hold pressurized gases under tremendous force. If they explode, they are capable of obliterating anything within their blast radius, the area of impact around a rocket. Korolev and von Braun both knew a good and reliable rocket could go bad. It wasn't a question of "if," but "when."

As von Braun struggled to perfect his Redstone rocket for Project Mercury, he didn't know Korolev was also suffering failures with his own crewed spaceflight program, Vostok. Despite a mounting list of space spectaculars, by October 1960, Korolev was back at his desk after an epic streak of bad luck at the test range.

"Over a period of ten months," remembered engineer Boris

Chertok, "there had been six failures. The spacecraft hadn't even made it into near-Earth orbit." And that wasn't his biggest problem. Khrushchev, hungry for more propaganda opportunities, expected Korolev to launch a Soviet cosmonaut into orbit in December—just two months away.

Korolev joked that the string of failures occurred because it was a leap year. Superstitious Russians believed leap years brought bad luck. The chief designer knew better, of course. The solution was always the same: more tests, data collection, and if necessary, redesign.

An exacting taskmaster, Korolev dazzled with his genius for managing the sprawling rocket manufacturing enterprise he supervised. He refused to tolerate carelessness. His team fell in lockstep with their leader. Delays were inevitable in big rocket manufacturing. That was the cost of doing business with the cosmos. But Korolev's work ethic did not protect him from rival engineers repeatedly pitching their own proposals to Soviet leadership. Korolev's greatest achievements were never enough to guarantee his position with Khruschchev.

Mikhail Yangel was the latest Russian rocket designer to step up and offer an alternative to Korolev's R-7, the Soviet Union's only intercontinental ballistic missile. A prominent figure in the Soviet space program, Yangel hoped his own rocket, the R-16, would replace Korolev's R-7 as the country's primary ICBM for defense.

Early in his career, Yangel had worked under Korolev, but he had quickly risen through the ranks. Then, during a particularly uncomfortable period in the early 1950s, Yangel was Korolev's superior. During those years, their working relationship was tense, both men possessing domineering personalities. They avoided one another when possible. Korolev preferred to communicate with Yangel through a deputy.

Korolev and Yangel maintained a "friendly rivalry" but parted ways on a fundamental design philosophy: fuel. Yangel's rocket engines burned a particularly nasty fuel comprised of hypergolic propellants—substances that catch fire when they come into contact with one another. Korolev distrusted the highly volatile fuel. He rightly called it "devil's venom." The fumes were capable of liquefying human organs. Korolev preferred the proven stability and reliability of liquid oxygen engines. But the hypergolic propellants in Yangel's rocket made it appealing to military leaders. It could be stored with a full tank of gas, reducing the amount of time it took to launch it. By contrast, Korolev's R-7 missile needed an entire day to fuel.

Yangel also received important high-level support for his R-16 rocket. When it came to rapid response to an enemy attack, the R-16 was the obvious choice for Marshal Mitrofan Nedelin, the commander-in-chief of the Strategic Missile Force. Khrushchev agreed that the R-16 could be a better choice than Korolev's rocket. The Soviet leader also believed fierce competition among his best designers would result in superior technology.

Yangel and Korolev had one important thing in common. The same man, Valentin Glushko, designed both their engines. The legendary engine designer threw his full support behind the R-16, breaking ranks with Korolev in favor of Yangel. Korolev was furious at Glushko's betrayal.

With Khrushchev and Nedelin's support, and Glushko designing his engine, Yangel stepped forward to challenge Korolev. If he succeeded, the chief designer's quest for the moon would be over.

On October 24, 1960, the day of Yangel's R-16 launch, Major General Aleksandr G. Mrykin was on duty. He headed for a bunker, about five hundred feet from the launch site, for a cigarette. Along the way, he spotted Yangel and asked the rocket designer to join him.

Yangel welcomed the invitation to step away from the hectic work happening around the rocket. The R-16 had been plagued by a string of pre-launch setbacks. The ground crew was well into their seventy-second hour of work, with Nedelin barking orders from his chair, fifty feet way from the rocket. There was no justification for the reckless pace. The launch was scheduled to coincide with the anniversary of the Russian Revolution; they were not under attack. But Nedelin insisted that Yangel make the deadline as promised. To save time, Nedelin reportedly said, "We'll modify the missile on the launchpad! The nation is waiting for us!"

Although experienced technicians knew how deadly a fueled rocket could be, they ignored safety precautions and put themselves in harm's way to satisfy Nedelin's outrageous and dangerous demands. Some milled around the base of the fully fueled R-16. Others perched on the gantry close to the rocket, high above the launchpad. Standing next to any fully fueled rocket was irresponsible in the extreme, and the R-16 was a temperamental metal beast with a bellyful of nasty, organ-dissolving chemicals.

Not long after Yangel and Mrykin stepped inside the bunker, an electrical error opened the valves of the rocket's second-stage engine.

The hypergolic fuel instantly ignited.

In less time than it took for Yangel to take a drag from his cigarette, the rocket's fuel tank detonated.

Yangel couldn't believe his eyes. A three-thousand-degree inferno raged at the launchpad. The men on the gantries were instantly incinerated. Anyone who could still stand, lungs choking in the poisonous gases, attempted to flee the conflagration. "People ran . . . toward the bunker," one witness reported. "But on this route was a strip of new-laid tar, which immediately melted. Many got stuck in the hot sticky mass and became victims of the fire." Another witness remembered that, "One man momentarily escaped from the fire but got tangled up in the barbed wire surrounding the launchpad. The next moment he, too, was engulfed in flames." Accepting the offer of a cigarette from Mrykin and entering the bunker had saved Yangel's life. Marshal Nedelin, seated close to the base of the rocket, had been killed instantly in the blast. His corpse was later recovered, but it was burned beyond recognition. Only a single gold star from his uniform verified his identity.

The Soviet government's reaction was to immediately classify the catastrophe and forbid survivors to speak about it. Russians had died senseless deaths in what amounted to a rushed and ill-advised publicity stunt. Khrushchev knew that failure on such a large scale would shatter the illusion of the powerful Soviet space program. In truth, it was not so advanced that it was foolproof. Total secrecy was the only way to shield the USSR from humiliation.

In official public statements, the cause of Nedelin's death was falsely reported as an aircraft accident. It wasn't until 1989, almost thirty years after it had happened, that the truth of the fire was declassified. For the first time, the facts were reported in the media and witnesses could speak openly about what they had seen. By that time, however, the Soviet Union was undergoing major political changes, and the revelation was overshadowed by more pressing current events.

In total, 126 people died in what would come to be known as the Nedelin disaster, named for the one man who could have prevented it.

CHAPTER 28

THE FIRST TO FLY

The American space program also kept secrets. Just as the Soviets covered up disasters and hid their failures, the United States tried to protect itself from ridicule, especially when it came to its astronauts. The Mercury Seven were portrayed as heroes, with untarnished reputations and the highest moral character. The image reassured the country that these men were trustworthy—a trait worth its weight in gold, since NASA depended on taxpayers for funding.

John Glenn believed that the Mercury Seven astronauts had a responsibility to the American people as role models, and he was not shy about voicing this opinion. His disciplined attitude earned Glenn the nickname "the Clean Marine" from his fellow astronauts. When Glenn discovered that Alan Shepard might be involved with women who were not his wife, he was outspoken in his disapproval. He argued that scandalous press reports could have serious repercussions for the space program. Shepard and some of the other astronauts didn't appreciate Glenn's criticism. They respected his spotless reputation and status as a celebrated war hero, but his candid opinions and rigid adherence to the rules of good behavior sometimes made him unpopular within the group.

By contrast, Alan Shepard was a wild card who liked to test boundaries by pushing them to the absolute limit, both in the cockpit and on the ground. It made him a daring and accomplished pilot, but it complicated his relationships, especially with Glenn. Shepard refused to play by the rules Glenn wanted to enforce. He knew that he was expected to look and act like a squeaky-clean hero for the television cameras. But behind the scenes, Alan Shepard wasn't a squeaky-clean guy who always cared what people thought. In fact, some of the astronauts felt as if they didn't know Shepard at all. One anonymously admitted, "You might think you'd get to know someone well after working so closely with him. . . . Well, it's not that way with Shepard. He's always holding something back." Shepard and Glenn both wanted the first Mercury flight and to become the first American in space. Shepard didn't bother hiding his ambition from anyone, especially John Glenn.

In January 1961, Bob Gilruth, head of NASA's Space Task Group, called a meeting with the astronauts and threw them a curveball. NASA would not select the first Mercury pilot—the astronauts would decide in a peer vote. Glenn was devastated. Shepard might have been distant and mysterious, but Glenn wore his strict opinions on his sleeve. He knew by that measure, he fell short.

When the votes were counted, the honor of the first Mercury flight eluded the Clean Marine. Although Glenn would later make spaceflight history as the first American to orbit the Earth on February 20, 1962, he was not chosen to be the first American to travel into space. Instead, his team chose a brash and unapologetic rule breaker. Alan Shepard, they agreed, was hands down the most talented pilot of the Mercury Seven. All he needed now was a ride.

Von Braun's modified Redstone was the rocket scheduled to carry Shepard into space, but its last test flight had been measured in inches instead of miles. Von Braun refused to allow an astronaut aboard until the rocket was proven safe. A three-year-old West African chimpanzee, known as Number 65, was selected to fly in yet another launch test. The animal had been trapped in the wild and sold to the US Air Force, who trained him, along with approximately forty other chimpanzees, for participation in the space program and life in captivity. Like the space dogs that paved the way toward human spaceflight for the Soviets, the chimpanzee's was the first life that would be risked in the Mercury program. Before his flight, it was decided that if Number 65 survived, he would be given a new name.

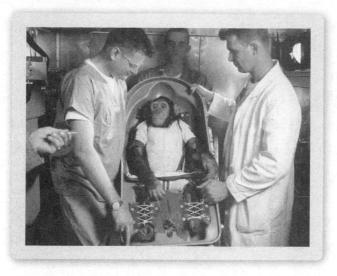

Chimp Number 65 (aka Astrochimp Ham) and a team of technicians prepare for launch.

Number 65 was placed in the primate capsule on top of the Redstone rocket and lifted off from Cape Canaveral on January 31, 1961. The poor chimp endured a troubled seventeen-minute flight. A valve malfunctioned, allowing too much fuel into the rocket's engine, causing the capsule to fly off course. Inside, temperatures rose to dangerous levels, threatening the chimp's life. The trip concluded with a splashdown in the Atlantic Ocean, but Number 65 was still in jeopardy, nearly drowning when salt water poured inside the capsule. The rescue helicopter arrived just in time. Unlike the Soviet space dog Laika, the chimp was safely recovered, and his flight was considered a success, despite the problems. Number 65 had narrowly survived but had earned his name, Astrochimp Ham, and a place in spaceflight history.

The test failed to convince von Braun that the Mercury-Redstone rocket was safe enough for Shepard's launch. The death of an astronaut at this stage could set the space program back for years, or destroy it altogether. President Kennedy's advisers agreed, also recommending additional test flights before approving the rocket for Alan Shepard's flight.

When Shepard heard the news, he was livid. He had beaten six of the best pilots in the world for the honor of being the first Mercury astronaut. He had endured painful medical tests, completed grueling survival training in the desert, and studied mechanical engineering, rocket systems, and astrophysics. He was a test pilot; risk came with the job—he was ready to go! He believed the delays were costing the United States time it didn't have. While America buried opportunity beneath miles of red tape, Shepard feared the Soviets would deliver them another crushing defeat.

CHAPTER 29

THE RUSSIANS' "RIGHT STUFF"

In the Soviet Union, cosmonaut Yuri Gagarin didn't look like he was trying to defeat much of anything as he lounged on a sofa in a Soviet medical center waiting room. Fellow cosmonaut Alexei Leonov recalled watching Gagarin relax that day with a copy of *The Old Man and the Sea* by Ernest Hemingway, one of the few American authors whose work had been translated into Russian. Hemingway's manly, larger-than-life characters personified the conventional image of strength and bravery valued in Russian culture. If Gagarin was nervous about his examination, it didn't show. The dark-haired, five-foot-two fighter pilot sat shirtless in pajama pants, calmly waiting for his turn. Like the Mercury 7 astronauts, the twenty men selected to be Soviet cosmonauts also endured invasive medical tests and rigorous training.

"Little Eagles"

The cosmonauts were well into their training by the time they were first introduced to the chief designer and learned his true identity.

"Hello, my little eagles!" Korolev said to the group.

"Hello!" the excited pilots replied, honored to finally meet the mysterious rocket engineer.

Korolev unfolded a sheet of paper listing their names as he inspected his first corps of cosmonauts. "He was looking at us with such intensity," Alexei Leonov later remembered. "It was as if he was looking through us. When he got to Gagarin's name, he asked about his parents, where he was from, everything." It was obvious that Korolev favored Gagarin.

The two men shared a similar background. They both came from proud, working-class families. As young men, both attended trade schools. Gagarin had a cheerful, outgoing personality, which Korolev also liked. More than that, he thought Gagarin *looked* like a stereotypical hero, with blue eyes and a bright smile. The cameras would love the grinning, charismatic young pilot with the easy laugh and unflappable attitude—qualities that could not be taught but were prized by Khrushchev. It came as no surprise that Korolev selected Gagarin to be the first cosmonaut in space.

Yuri and the Devil

Yuri Alexeyevich Gagarin's resilient spirit first emerged during boyhood. He was born on March 9, 1934, in the village of Klushino, a hundred miles from Moscow. His parents, Alexei and Anna, worked on one of Stalin's state-owned collective farms and struggled to keep food on the table for Yuri; his older brother, Valentin; his youngest brother, Boris; and his sister, Zoya.

By October 1941, the Nazis had invaded the Soviet Union and occupied Klushino. They seized the Gagarins' house and forced the family from their home. The six Gagarins had no choice but to seek shelter in their *zemlianka* next to their house. Russians used these makeshift dugouts for storage. Inside the crude outbuilding, the family slept on the ground, which they covered with straw.

One day, Yuri and Valentin witnessed a wounded Russian colonel being interrogated by two German soldiers. The dying man gestured for the officers to approach him. When they were close, he detonated a hand grenade. The colonel was dead, but he had taken his two interrogators with him.

Yuri never forgot this act of heroism and resistance. He longed to be a hero too, and the young Gagarin brothers sought payback against the Nazis. The three boys, Yuri (age eight), Boris (age six), and Valentin (age eighteen), along with other village children, collected all the glass they could find and broke it into pieces, scattering it along the roads frequented by German military vehicles. Then the junior saboteurs hid behind bushes along the roadside to watch as large German supply trucks rolled over the glass and their tires exploded.

The children's resistance activities attracted the attention of a particularly cruel Gestapo official, whom they nicknamed the Devil. The Devil rightly suspected that the Gagarin brothers were among the troublemakers.

Sometime later, with the promise of a chocolate bar, the Devil lured the youngest Gagarin brother, Boris, closer to him. Boris reached for the chocolate and the officer stomped on his small hand. Boris wept and his fingers bled. Using the scarf Boris wore, the soldier hanged him from a nearby apple tree. As the terrified child gasped and choked, the man laughed and took photographs. When Boris's mother, Anna, arrived on the scene and fought to save her son, the Devil pointed his rifle it at her. Just as he was about to fire, he was called away by an officer. Anna managed to rescue her son from the tree. He was still alive, but the ordeal left him unable to walk for a month after the incident, and the child suffered nightmares thereafter.

The attempted murder of his little brother enraged Yuri, who redoubled his attacks against the Nazis. He shoved dirt into the tailpipes of their vehicles, destroying the valuable equipment. The Devil searched everywhere, promising to kill Yuri if he found him. But he never got the chance. He was transferred from the village before he could make good on the threat. The Gagarin children and their parents survived the war, and Yuri had discovered what it meant to be a hero.

•　•　•

In the Soviet space program, though, being a hero could be deadly. Like the American astronauts, the cosmonauts knew and accepted the danger. As Gagarin finalized preparations to become the Soviet Union's first person in space, other members of the cosmonaut corps were training for future missions. In late March 1961, Valentin Bondarenko was confined to a locked and soundproof pressure chamber as part of a routine fifteen-day exercise. He was removing medical sensors from his body and cleaning those areas with a piece of alcohol-soaked cloth. He tossed it aside, failing to notice that the fabric had landed on a nearby hot plate and burst into flames. The oxygen inside the chamber ignited. By the time a technician noticed the blaze, the chamber, with Bondarenko trapped inside, was engulfed in flames. The technician frantically tried to open the door, but it was pressure sealed and took several minutes to open. By the time Bondarenko was finally pulled from the fire, his body was horribly burned, but he was still alive. "It was my fault," he reportedly said over and over again. "No one else is to blame." He died hours later in the hospital.

Whether or not any of the other cosmonauts knew about Bondarenko's death at the time remains unclear. As it had with the Nedelin disaster, the Soviet government concealed his tragic death until 1986.

CHAPTER 30

"POYEKHALI!"
("LET'S GO!")

April 12, 1961

A few weeks after Bondarenko died, Yuri Gagarin was ready to risk his life in an attempt to become the first person in space. At liftoff, he could be heard shouting, *"Poyekhali!"* ("Let's go!") from inside the Vostok 1 spacecraft as it rose from the launchpad. Flight doctors monitoring Gagarin's vital signs in the minutes before liftoff noted his heart rate was a relaxed sixty-five beats per minute.

Four minutes into the flight, the chief designer spoke to his cosmonaut from the ground.

"Everything is normal. How do you feel?" Korolev asked.

"I feel excellent, in a good mood," said Gagarin.

"Good boy! Excellent! Everything is going well."

Gagarin reported that his visibility was good. "I see the clouds . . . It's beautiful!"

Yuri Gagarin (left) and Sergei Korolev (right).

Yuri Gagarin orbited the Earth for 108 minutes. As he prepared for reentry, the Vostok was scheduled to detach from its rear equipment module. The two parts of the spacecraft separated, but a tangle of electrical wiring prevented a full detachment. The capsule struggled against the weight of the attached equipment module, hurtling Gagarin's Vostok toward the Earth's atmosphere at a deadly angle. As his spacecraft spiraled violently out of control, Gagarin almost passed out.

Miraculously, the cable connection severed on its own, and Gagarin safely ejected from the capsule and floated to Earth by parachute, one hour and forty-eight minutes after he had lifted off, having traveled a total of twenty-five thousand miles.

Gagarin later received full honors in Moscow's Red Square. Thousands crowded the streets. Korolev watched as his fellow Russians cheered with pride for Gagarin's accomplishment. As the cosmonaut waved and smiled, basking in the glory of so much admiration, Korolev viewed the scene in secret from inside an unmarked car in the motorcade to protect his identity. He listened as his countrymen chanted "Gagarin!" while Korolev's name remained top secret.

CHAPTER 31

"LIGHT THIS CANDLE"

"It is a most impressive scientific accomplishment," President Kennedy said of Gagarin's achievement. "And also I think that we, all of us, as members of the race, have the greatest admiration for the Russian who participated in this extraordinary feat." Kennedy had been asleep while Yuri Gagarin's Vostok 1 capsule orbited the Earth. For some time, American intelligence reports had suggested that a manned Soviet launch was in the works. Jerome Wiesner, Kennedy's science adviser, had briefed him on the night of April 11 that the launch appeared to be imminent, and the president accepted that it would likely happen and asked not to be awakened.

Kennedy was more willing to invest in space exploration than his conservative predecessor, Dwight Eisenhower. In March, he had received an additional funding request from NASA admnistrator James Webb for two projects: a space capsule development program called Apollo and a new rocket, the Saturn. The three-stage Saturn vehicle that would be used to carry the Apollo capsule into space would be a monster, standing 363 feet—60 feet taller than the Statue of Liberty—and weighing as much as a battle cruiser. Kennedy hesitated to commit additional money to both projects at the time, agreeing only to fund the Saturn. However, Gagarin's successful flight raised the stakes for JFK. America was losing to the Russians. Kennedy summoned key advisers to the White House— James Webb and Hugh Dryden from NASA, budget director David Bell, and science adviser Jerome Wiesner—to discuss the country's chances of still winning the space race. The general consensus was that an American victory was feasible. However, the cost was estimated at $40 billion.

Eight days after Gagarin made world history as the first human being in space, Kennedy sent a letter to vice president Lyndon Johnson, who was also head of the National Aeronautics and Space Council:

> *Do we have a chance of beating the Soviets by putting a laboratory in space, or by a trip around the moon, or by a rocket to land on the moon, or by a rocket to go to the moon and back with a man? Is there any other space program which promises dramatic results in which we could win?*

Johnson read the president's letter and wrote to America's biggest champion of space travel, the man who had been hoping for a shot at the moon since he had first set foot in the desert at Fort Bliss, Texas, in 1945. Von Braun was elated. After sixteen years, Washington was finally asking the right questions.

Von Braun answered Johnson's letter:

> *We have an excellent chance of beating the Soviets to the first landing of a crew on the moon. While today we do not have such a rocket, it is unlikely that the Soviets have it. Therefore, we would not have to enter the race toward this obvious next goal in space exploration against hopeless odds favoring the Soviets. With an all-out crash program I think we could accomplish this objective in 1967/68.*

By "crash program" von Braun also meant *cash* program. Getting to the moon wouldn't be cheap, nor would it be easy. In many ways, the American space program was in its infancy. The Soviets were ahead after the Gagarin launch, and America had yet to prove that it could launch an astronaut and safely return him to Earth.[7]

---

7 Neither Kennedy nor his successor, Lyndon B. Johnson, knew about von Braun's complicity in the crimes committed at Mittelwerk. The truth would not be discovered for another twenty years, after both former presidents had died.

Shepard Makes History

May 5, 1961

Six days after von Braun replied to Johnson, Alan Shepard was waiting patiently inside the cramped Mercury 3 space capsule atop von Braun's modified Redstone rocket. His moment had finally arrived. Three weeks earlier, Shepard's fear that a Soviet cosmonaut would beat America into space had come true. The astronaut knew he had something to prove and that his country was counting on him.

Each of the Mercury astronauts named their space capsule. Shepard christened his *Freedom 7*. He wore a silvery, skintight space suit that looked like something out of a science-fiction film. The suit

Mercury Seven astronaut Alan Shepard in his silver pressurized suit and helmet, as he prepares to become the first American in space.

was so snug that the astronaut required assistance wriggling into it. Shepard had broken out in a sweat from the exertion. Even something as simple as getting dressed for the flight was a team effort, but only one person would sit on top of von Braun's missile and blast into space.

Shepard was ready. He wanted to go. But more than that, he *needed to go.*

To the bathroom.

The orange juice and coffee from his preflight breakfast made him increasingly uncomfortable. He tried not to think about it, but there was nowhere for him to "go." There was barely enough room in the capsule for him, let alone a toilet. The astronauts joked that a pilot didn't fly the Mercury—he wore it. Unlike Gagarin, who orbited the Earth, Shepard's simpler mission would be another suborbital flight, meaning he would fly up and back down again. From liftoff to splashdown, it would only take fifteen minutes. After strapping into the capsule, the flight delays began. Before Shepard knew it, he had been waiting for more than three hours.

As time passed, Shepard's full bladder was becoming a serious preflight problem, and he radioed ground control to report a status update.

Fellow Mercury Seven astronaut Gordon Cooper, stationed in the nearby blockhouse, took the call when he heard Shepard's voice through his headset.

"Man, I got to pee," Shepard said to Cooper. "Check and see if I can get out quickly and relieve myself." Cooper relayed the request, but the engineers hadn't anticipated something like this. They didn't have a full-bladder contingency plan. Removing the astronaut from the capsule was not an option, according to von Braun. It would take longer to escort Shepard to the bathroom and remove his space suit than to launch and land *Freedom 7*. The delay could result in the scrubbing of the flight altogether. Cooper relayed the bad news. He would have to hold it. Shepard responded with a suggestion that he be allowed to relieve himself in his space suit. Again, the request was denied. None of the engineers knew what would happen if liquid was introduced into the capsule environment. Would it short-circuit electronics? Electrocute the astronaut? The safest option was for him to wait.

As minutes ticked by, the try-to-hold-it strategy weakened along with Shepard's bladder. Finally, without another alternative, the engineers permitted the astronaut to relieve himself in the space suit. Physically, Shepard felt better, and none of the engineers' fears came to pass. But Shepard's patience, like the urine soaking his space suit, eventually evaporated. "Why don't you fix your little problem and light this candle," he snapped.

After four tense hours on the launchpad and one unscheduled bladder release, Shepard blasted off. Forty-five million Americans gawked at their televisions as the rocket hurtled Shepard's capsule into the sky. *Freedom 7* traveled 116 miles before dropping safely into the Atlantic Ocean fifteen minutes later. The country rejoiced. Shepard was the first American to leave Earth. He had not matched Gagarin's technical achievement by orbiting the planet, but he had renewed America's confidence that it could win the space race.

Three weeks after Shepard's flight, on May 25, Kennedy addressed a special joint session of Congress and announced his plans for America's future in space.

"These are extraordinary times and we face an extraordinary challenge," he said. "Our strength as well as our convictions have imposed upon this nation the role of leader in freedom's cause."

In a conference room at the Marshall Space Flight Center in Huntsville, von Braun and his closest associates listened to Kennedy's remarks.

"Now it is time to take longer strides," Kennedy said. "Time for a great new American enterprise. Time for this nation to take a clearly leading role in space achievement, which in many ways may hold the key to our future on Earth. . . . I believe that this nation should commit itself to achieving the goal, before this decade is out, of landing a man on the moon and returning him safely to the Earth." Upon hearing Kennedy's announcement of the deadline, the Huntsville conference room burst into cheers and applause. "No single space project in this period will be more impressive to mankind or more important for the long-range exploration of space," Kennedy said. "And none will be so difficult or expensive to accomplish."

The following year, on September 12, 1962, President Kennedy delivered an iconic speech of his presidency, "We Choose to Go to the Moon," on the Rice University campus in Houston, Texas. The moment cemented America's commitment to landing a man on the moon within ten years. His rallying cry set the tone for the decade. Von Braun knew the challenge that lay ahead of him and everyone at NASA. It was an ambitious schedule, but he was elated. Wernher von Braun had finally earned his moon shot.

Kennedy's ten-year timetable injected the space program with enthusiasm and an infusion of cash. The NASA annual budget dramatically increased, totaling $5 billion by 1966. In response to the demands of the moon shot, aerospace industry development exploded around the US as NASA facilities in Florida, Houston, and Huntsville expanded. The space agency had only ten years to figure how to accomplish the seemingly impossible. When Kennedy's countdown began on Project Apollo, most of the technology required for achieving his goal had not been invented. Apollo was a NASA project, but the agency employed subcontractors to complete specific tasks: small-town textile mills in South Carolina manufactured fabric for space suits, and aerospace engineering giants with names like Rocketdyne manufactured the rocket's engines. More than four hundred thousand Americans all across the country dedicated their skills to Project Apollo.

A Soviet Moon Rocket

America's overwhelming—and public—commitment of resources to the Apollo program did not go unnoticed by Korolev. What the United States and the Russian people didn't know, however, was that Korolev also had plans for a moon rocket, the N-1: a thirty-five-story giant weighing as much as four hundred double-decker buses. The project had been approved two weeks before Kennedy's Rice University speech, with a hefty price tag to match. The estimated cost of manufacturing and launching ten of the rockets was 457 million rubles. Korolev knew he faced an uphill battle for funding.[8]

As the prospect of Korolev's N-1 brought him closer to his dream of space travel, his past came back to haunt him in the form of two old rivals: Valentin Glushko and Mikhail Yangel. Korolev felt that Glushko had betrayed him by working with Yangel on the R-16 (the rocket that had exploded during the Nedelin disaster), but he also knew Glushko was the Soviet Union's best rocket-engine designer. Yet when Korolev approached him about building the engines for the N-1, he found himself in unpleasant but familiar territory. Glushko still insisted upon using the hypergolic fuels known as "devil's venom." Korolev was adamant in his refusal. Once again, the rivals vehemently disagreed.

Instead, Korolev chose Nikolai Kuznetsov, a skilled airplane engine designer who had never built a rocket engine. Kuznetsov

---

8 The actual cost of the N-1 would be four billion rubles.

proposed powering the huge N-1 rocket by clustering its engines. Whereas von Braun's Saturn V had a cluster of five engines in its first stage, Kuznestov recommended thirty. The Soviets would have to choreograph the simultaneous firing of *six times* as many engines as the Saturn V. The only way to ensure success on that scale would be repeated and costly engine tests before launching. But there was no money to build a test stand for the thirty-engine cluster. The designer wouldn't know if the engines worked until they were fired on launch day.

Meanwhile, Mikhail Yangel had gone to Khrushchev and proposed a moon rocket of his own. Although his R-16 had exploded in the Nedelin disaster, Yangel remained a prominent and respected engineer. Without a focused moon-landing program, like Apollo, Khrushchev wasn't motivated to concentrate all funding on a single rocket project. Instead, he also awarded money to Yangel—robbing Korolev of funds he desperately needed for the N-1.

It must have frustrated Korolev to watch von Braun's adopted country unite behind his glittering Apollo moon-landing project. For Korolev, the fight to build a comparable program in the USSR was like trying to construct a house of cards in a hurricane. The force of gravity was easier for him to overcome than the politics involved in securing enough money for his work.

CHAPTER 32

BEHIND THE WALL

As Korolev and von Braun raced to the moon, the political and philosophical differences between democracy in the United States and communism in the Soviet Union were about to divide a country and create a new battlefront in the Cold War.

On August 13, 1961, Peter Guba, an eighteen-year-old police officer in East Berlin, was watching television at his mother's house. A news report announced that a barbed-wire fence was being erected around West Berlin to isolate it not only from Soviet-controlled East Berlin but also from the surrounding East Germany. Travel between the two parts of the city was forbidden. Before the construction of the wall, East Germans had been free to travel between East and West German-held territories. Gradually, millions of young and educated East Germans fled to the west. With the loss of its workforce, East Germany faced financial collapse. The Berlin Wall would stop defections, trap East Germans behind it, and eliminate the influence of democratic ideas. It would also cruelly separate East and West German families and friends for decades.

As the barbed wire was rolled into the streets, Guba's job as a police officer expanded overnight. He became a border guard, expected to defend East Berlin by deadly force if necessary. His orders included stopping anyone who tried to escape or illegally cross the hastily constructed barrier that was eventually reinforced with concrete. The area between the divided cities, known as "the death strip," became a no-man's land riddled with more than a million land mines. Armed guards like Guba were stationed along the perimeter in one of the wall's 302 guard towers and ordered to shoot anyone who attempted to cross. "We felt like wild animals trapped in a cage," he remembered decades later, "like evil creatures that were just waiting to pounce."

The Berlin Wall did benefit one person, albeit accidentally. Both the Mittelwerk and the former Peenemünde rocket factories were located in what became communist-held East Germany. Defended by armed East German guards like Peter Guba, the concrete-and-barbed-wire barricade further isolated von Braun's Nazi past from his new life in America.

In the Soviet Union, Korolev felt the walls closing around him as he followed events in America with growing concern. He watched Alan Shepard's historic flight. He heard Kennedy's announcement about Project Apollo, which would land a man on the moon within the decade. And then, on February 20, 1962, he saw John Glenn become the first American astronaut to successfully orbit the Earth thirty times in the *Friendship 7* Mercury capsule. It was a turning point. The Americans were catching up because they had more money and a strategic plan to reach the moon. The Soviet Union lacked both. President Kennedy had put the full weight of the White House behind the American moon shot. When it came to the Soviet space program, however, Khrushchev valued high-profile space spectaculars more than advancing the science of spaceflight. Korolev was expected to accomplish both goals and always without enough funding.

The enormous stress of Korolev's daily life compromised his health. His body had never fully recovered from years of torture in the Gulag, but he powered through discomfort, refusing to slow his exhausting pace. It was not uncommon for him to work eighteen-hour days for weeks at a time. He obsessed over the tiniest details, insisting on personally supervising every facet of his huge rocket organization. The chief designer had been relentless in his pursuit of spaceflight since Gagarin's launch, with the flights of Vostok 2, 3, and 4. Inevitably, the relentless workload, combined with Korolev's stubborn refusal to take better care of his health, caught up with him.

By August 1962, Korolev was admitted to the hospital with intestinal bleeding and unbearable pain. He was hospitalized for weeks under close observation. Doctors ordered him to take time off to rest. He agreed but continued to work from his bed because

Khrushchev had asked Korolev for another Vostok launch. The Soviet leader wanted to respond to John Glenn's Earth-orbiting mission with another defining "first" in spaceflight.

Korolev's next mission would stun the world, because his newest cosmonaut . . . was a woman.

CHAPTER 33

"SHE IS A GAGARIN IN A SKIRT"

June 16, 1963

Baikonur Cosmodrome, Kazakhstan

"You're working the communications excellently," the chief designer said to his cosmonaut from ground control, "like a solid communicator with twenty years of experience. Do your work well, excellently, that's what we need in space."

"Everything is normal. I remember our arrangement," the twenty-six-year-old cosmonaut, Valentina Tereshkova, replied, adding, "I'm not a delicate lady."

Korolev had recovered and was in ground control when Tereshkova prepared to lift off from the Baikonur Cosmodrome. Fellow cosmonaut Valery Bykovsky had been in orbit aboard his Vostok 5 capusle for two days. Tereshkova would launch and join Bykovsky in orbit aboard her Vostok 6, their separate spacecraft at times traveling within three miles of each other. If she succeeded, Tereshkova would become the first woman in space. Yet no one outside the Soviet space program knew she was there that day—not even her mother. Tereshkova's family had no idea she had been training for over a year as a cosmonaut. She was sworn to secrecy.[9]

The first and youngest woman in space, Valentina Tereshkova.

Tereshkova was just eighteen years old when she strapped on a parachute and threw herself out of an airplane for the first time. It was a life-changing moment for a teenage farm girl from the Yaroslavl region of Russia who worked in a textile mill. She enjoyed jumping so much it became a hobby. After leaping from the plane, she waited "as

9 The Soviets had a history of recruiting female pilots. The USSR was the first nation to allow women to fly in combat during World War II. However, due to the extreme secrecy around the Soviet space program, many details were classified.

long as possible before pulling the cord, just to feel the air" for forty to fifty breathtaking seconds of free fall as the ground raced toward her. Before long, the familiar weight of the chute was as natural to her as a pair of wings to a seabird. When it unfurled high above her head, she floated. The feeling, she said, "was marvelous." Valentina Tereshkova wasn't afraid to fall. She knew she was born to fly.

Tereshkova and four other talented female skydivers were chosen from a list of four hundred women candidates. Skydiving experience was critical. The only way for a cosmonaut to exit a Vostok capsule was to "punch out," a dangerous maneuver initiated by activating the craft's ejection seat at an altitude of more than four miles, after it reentered Earth's atmosphere. Once the cosmonaut was clear of the capsule, she opened her parachute.

Tereshkova's call sign was Chayka—"the seagull."

Nikolai Kamanin, deputy chief of the air force, supervised the selection and training of cosmonauts, including Tereshkova and the other female candidates. Kamanin expected the women to overcome an obstacle that did not challenge their male colleagues: they had to prove they could do the job in spite of the fact that they were female. Kamanin's journal highlighted the unfair double standard used to evaluate the trailblazing Russian women who were willing to die to prove that human spaceflight was possible. In one entry, he criticized a candidate who enjoyed "taking walks (although she has a husband and four-year-old son)." He seemed to believe that her enjoyment of this light exercise took away from time she should have spent caring for her family. By contrast, a journal entry about Tereshkova praised her abilities but still managed to be blatantly sexist:

"We must first send Tereshkova into space flight. Tereshkova, she is a Gagarin in a skirt."

Of course Valentina Tereshkova was not wearing a skirt when she fearlessly blasted off from the Baikonur Cosmodrome in June 1963; she was outfitted in the same Soviet space suit that male cosmonauts wore, and for the most part, the launch had gone according to plan. By the end of the first day, however, Tereshkova suffered from motion sickness and vomited. Korolev considered aborting the flight early, but the Seagull reported that she felt better and asked that the flight continue. She reassured ground control that she would fulfill her duties and remember all that she had learned. The Seagull was determined to keep flying.

Valentina Tereshkova's achievement was bittersweet for the other four female cosmonauts. Tatyana D. Kuznetsova (age twenty), Valentina L. Ponomareva (age twenty-eight), Irina B. Solovyova (age twenty-four), and Zhanna D. Yerkina (age twenty-two) knew there would be only one Vostok mission for a woman. Unlike Tereshkova, none of their names would appear in the press. There would be no interviews, parades, or public celebration. Tereshkova's flight had been a stunt, not a statement in favor of equality. Nonetheless, Soviet news outlets heralded her achievement as a victory for their country. The first woman in space was a Russian, not an American.

Tereshkova knew that to Khrushchev, her flight was just another spectacular victory in his publicity war against the West. The Soviet space program appeared so advanced *even a woman* could be sent successfully into orbit. It's likely that all the women who submitted themselves for consideration as cosmonauts would have cared less about this distinction and more about the prospect of flying into space. They knew that men dominated the times in which they lived and that an opportunity like this came along once in a lifetime. They didn't argue the politics. It was a chance to serve their country. For Tereshkova, it was also a way to honor her late father, who had died in the fight against Hitler. For the world's first woman in space, it had been personal.

During her first and only spaceflight, Valentina Tereshkova orbited the Earth forty-eight times in three days. As she circled the planet over and over, the Seagull broadcast a message of hope and sisterhood. "Women of the world," she said. "Greetings to you from space. I wish you good luck and success." To this day, Tereshkova remains the youngest woman ever to have flown in space.

Both Vostok 5 and 6 landed safely on June 19, 1963, three hours apart.[10]

AMERICA'S FIRST WOMAN IN SPACE

It took the US two decades to catch up to the Soviet Union's launch of a woman into space. On June 18, 1983, Sally Ride became the first American woman aboard the space shuttle *Challenger*. She was thirty-two years old.

---

10 Valentina Tereshkova logged more hours in space than all six American Mercury flights combined.

CHAPTER 34

"THE PRESIDENT HAS BEEN SHOT"

On November 22, 1963, American television and radio stations interrupted their regular broadcasts with breaking news: President Kennedy was dead. Lee Harvey Oswald had fired three shots at forty-six-year-old Kennedy's open-air convertible as he rode with his wife, Jacqueline Kennedy, in a motorcade through Dealey Plaza in downtown Dallas. Vice President Lyndon B. Johnson was immediately sworn in as president of the United States. America, and the entire world, was in shock.

In the Soviet Union, Korolev was at home when he heard the news. His English-language expert, Vladimir Shevalyov, called him to report that the American president had been assassinated. Korolev lived with the constant suspicion that his phone was tapped by Soviet intelligence services. He knew it was inappropriate and potentially dangerous to speak favorably about the United States. Criticism of the Americans was expected in political circles. It was only in private that one could admire the US and the chief designer felt the loss of President Kennedy as well. Despite the risk, Korolev made no attempt to conceal the sorrow in his voice when he heard the tragic news. Shevalyov later revealed that he had "never heard Korolev criticize America."

In Huntsville, von Braun was devastated. He had grown fond of President Kennedy and respected his enthusiasm and support for the space program. He had met with the president on November 16, six days before he was assassinated.

November 16, 1963. NASA associate administrator for manned space flight George Mueller discusses the Saturn V with von Braun, President Kennedy, and other officials at Cape Canaveral.

On the day of Kennedy's funeral, von Braun's secretary, Bonnie Holmes, recalled him saying, "What a waste. What a tragic loss of a friend and a great leader." Holmes later said it was the only time she ever saw her boss cry.

Two months after Kennedy's death, von Braun wrote a letter to his widow, Jacqueline. He offered his condolences and shared some good news of successful launch tests he knew would have pleased her late husband. "Like for so many, the sad news from Dallas was a terrible personal blow to me," he wrote.

Several days later, he received Mrs. Kennedy's handwritten response: "What a wonderful world it was for a few years—with men like you to help realize his dreams for this country. . . . It is

Wernher von Braun (middle) and President John F. Kennedy (right) met on November 16, 1963.

my only consolation that at least he was given time to do some great work on this earth, which now seems such a miserable place without him."

In the wake of Kennedy's death, the moon shot became a memorial to the fallen American president and Cape Canaveral was renamed Cape Kennedy.[11]

---

11 Cape Canaveral was known as Cape Kennedy until 1973, when its original name was reinstated.

CHAPTER 35

STEPPING-STONES TO THE MOON

Work on the Apollo mission continued. The successful launches of Shepard, Glenn, Gagarin, Tereshkova, and others on Projects Mercury and Vostok proved it was possible for a human being to orbit the Earth in a single-person capsule. If either country was going to land on the moon, they needed to answer basic questions about prolonged missions lasting days or weeks. What would happen to astronauts who spent extended periods of time in orbit? How could they exit their spacecraft to "walk" in space? What was the best way to connect two separate spacecraft?

Project Gemini

To answer these questions, NASA undertook Project Gemini (Latin for "twins"). The Gemini capsule, based on the Mercury design, was expanded to seat two astronauts. According to NASA, the vehicle would test "long-duration flight, rendezvous and docking, and other techniques needed for journeys to the moon." The Gemini capsules would be launched with the air force's Titan II rocket, and the project would be managed by NASA's Manned Spaceflight Center in Houston. Von Braun's team wasn't responsible for building and launching every space capsule and rocket. NASA divided this heavy workload among different and specialized departments that all supported the primary goal of landing on the moon. Von Braun's focus was overseeing development of the Saturn V rocket for the Apollo moon-landing missions.

Voskhod Program

In the Soviet Union, Korolev and his team were in the early stages of designing their own two-person space capsule, called Soyuz. Korolev hoped that it could be modified to accommodate multiple cosmonauts for trips to space, and one day, to the moon.

Then, as if on cue, Nikita Khrushchev called in an order for another space spectacular, this time the "launch of three cosmonauts, right away!"

Three cosmonauts? The Americans were still trying to launch two, and Korolev's two-person Soyuz capsule was still in the design phase. He didn't have a capsule that was big enough to accommodate three cosmonauts wearing bulky space suits. The only available vehicle was the tiny Vostok capsule, which seated one person. In the past, Korolev had managed to pull rabbits out of hats, like a magician. However, Khrushchev seemed to believe that rabbits *lived* in hats—that he had only to ask, and Korolev would pull off another engineering miracle. Once more, with a shoestring budget and brazen ingenuity, Korolev and his team set out to accomplish the impossible.

The mission was a risky, fly-by-the-seat-of-their-pants-and-hope-for-the-best project from day one. They gutted the Vostok capsule to make room for three cosmonauts and renamed it Voskhod. The only way to squeeze two more cosmonauts inside the cramped capsule was by eliminating two safety features: space suits and ejection seats. The space suits provided the cosmonauts' oxygen. Now the entire capsule would have to be perfectly sealed to preserve the crew's air supply. Without ejection seats, there was no way to evacuate the Voskhod if something went wrong.

Landing the Voskhod after it reentered Earth's orbit was equally dangerous. During previous missions, the cosmonauts ejected and parachuted to safety. Now engineers had to figure out how to land the capsule softly with three cosmonauts inside. They settled on a reentry system comprised of retro-rockets and two parachutes working together to slow the capsule's descent and gently lower it to the ground. They ran the risk of the rockets igniting the parachutes' fabric during a landing, but Korolev decided the fire risk was minimal and he needed to make this flight happen. The chief designer's goal remained a rocket to the moon. Without the

Soviet leader's consistent and generous support, he would never get the chance to build it.

The F-1: A "Big Dumb Engine"

While Korolev secretly retooled his single-person Vostok space capsule into a flying sardine can for three cosmonauts, von Braun struggled to perfect the engine design for the future Apollo moon landing.

At the Marshall Space Flight Center, the F-1 was known as the "big dumb engine" because it used two common propellants: kerosene and liquid oxygen. It was an engineering masterpiece. It was also enormous: 18.5 feet tall, a diameter of 12.2 feet, weighing 20,000 pounds. The dome of the bell-shaped engine was covered by a large plate with thousands of tiny holes in its surface. It looked like a supersize showerhead. Fuel sprayed through the holes and into the engine bell at the rate of three tons per second; there it ignited, creating hot gases. As the gases were forced from the engine bell, the rocket rose off the ground.

The trouble was, the big dumb engine had an annoying habit of blowing up. In rocket engine design, it's called combustion instability. But F-1 engineers were unable to determine the precise cause of the instability. In test after test, the engine incinerated itself. Designers took a radical step by inserting a small bomb inside the F-1, hoping to balance the instability. It worked. Without knowledge of what caused the instability in the first place, however, it was impossible to guarantee the engine would not blow up again.

• • •

In the Soviet Union, Korolev's hastily remodeled three-person Voskhod was ready for its flight, but nonstop work on the project aggravated his ongoing health issues. He had been hospitalized twice, once for ten days with a heart complication, from which he recovered, but he returned to the hospital one week later due to a painful gall-bladder attack.

Shortly thereafter, Korolev learned that the N-1 moon rocket program was out of money, and that there were no plans to commit additional funds. Khrushchev had never fully endorsed a long-term moon-landing project. Most of the defense budget was earmarked for the building of ICBMs and nuclear weapons, not "civilian" space systems. Every facility dedicated to the production of the N-1 closed. Korolev refused to accept that his dream of a moon shot was dead. He fought for the N-1, campaigning for the program by writing letters to anyone who had enough power to reverse the decision and authorize more money. "The scope and progress of the work on 'big space' in the USA is a reason for great alarm," he warned, stressing the incredible power of von Braun's rocket to lift a heavy payload and orbit the Earth. "In this, the USA has already surpassed the Soviet Union."

The fight was far from over for Korolev, who was about to astonish the world again. Between fall 1964 and late winter 1965, his Voskhod capsule flights began. What had originally been a single-person vehicle had been modified to fit three cosmonauts . . .

barely. Without ejection seats or space suits, cosmonauts Konstantin Feoktistov, Vladimir Komarov, and Boris Yegorov were crammed inside the crowded capsule and launched on October 12, 1964. After one day in orbit, the crew prepared for reentry. It was a dangerous moment for the Voskhod. If the exterior of their spacecraft became severely damaged during their fiery trip through Earth's atmosphere, the cosmonauts had no space suits to protect their bodies from the heat or to provide oxygen. Mercifully, the capsule withstood reentry. Its parachutes deployed and the Voskhod drifted smoothly to the ground. In fact, the landing was so soft only the sound of brush against the capsule signaled to the cosmonauts they had touched down.

Although Korolev had beaten America to another historic first, no one in the US knew the truth. It had not been a step toward a Soviet moon landing, but another of Khruschev's propaganda stunts intended to undermine American confidence and boost Soviet prestige. It worked like a charm. The Soviets' policy of absolute secrecy created an information vacuum that people rushed to fill with frightening (and false) possibilities, including one theory that the Voskhod could be as powerful as NASA's Apollo vehicle. It wasn't, of course. But just five months later, before the US could catch its breath, or launch a Gemini flight with a two-person crew, Korolev would strike again.

On March 18, 1965, cosmonaut Alexei Leonov attempted another risky and ambitious mission: the world's first-ever space walk. Everything was going according to plan in the history-making flight. While cosmonaut Pavel Belyayev waited inside their Voskhod 2 spacecraft, Leonov put on his space suit and exited through the capsule's air lock. For twenty-three minutes and forty-one seconds, he floated in space from a sixteen-foot cable as their ship whirled around the Earth at seventeen thousand miles per hour.

The trouble began when Leonov attempted to reenter the capsule.

He immediately noticed the pressure inside his space suit had increased so much that he felt like he had shrunk inside it. His hands and feet had pulled away from his gloves and boots. He was unable to control his fingers. Leonov knew that it would be difficult, if not impossible, to use his hands and feet to pull himself back inside the spacecraft with the pressure building inside his suit. "It was taking far longer than it was supposed to," Leonov recalled years later, but he knew panic at this stage would be deadly. If he had any hope of fitting through the air lock, he would have to vent some of the pressure from his space suit. It was a dangerous maneuver. Leonov risked running out of air, or triggering decompression sickness—in which air bubbles that form in the bloodstream cause coma or death. He didn't have a choice. Thousands of miles below, a helpless Korolev waited as Leonov fought for his life. "My temperature was rising dangerously high," Leonov wrote. The exertion was taking a toll on the cosmonaut.

After twelve minutes, the determined Leonov finally squeezed back inside the air lock. With the emptiness of space now safely on the other side of the hatch, Leonov removed his helmet, "drenched with sweat, my heart racing."

Alexei Leonov photographed outside his Voskhod 2 spacecraft, performing humankind's first-ever space walk in 1965.

Once Leonov was safely back inside the capsule with Belyayev, the mission continued. The cosmonauts soon discovered they had another problem. The Voskhod 2's automatic landing program malfunctioned. They would have to manually land their capsule. Without the program, it was difficult to pinpoint the landing coordinates, but the pair managed to touch down unharmed. The spacecraft, however, had landed in the deep snow of remote Siberia, approximately 1,200 miles from their intended target. Their situation was precarious and deteriorating rapidly. The cosmonauts were vulnerable to predators. "We had only one pistol aboard our spacecraft, but plenty of ammunition," Leonov recalled. The rugged terrain made an airlift impossible, and a supply helicopter was dispatched to the Voskhod, dropping warm clothes and food to sustain the cosmonauts until a rescue party arrived. "As the sky darkened, the trees started cracking with the drop in temperature . . . and the wind began to howl." The temperature fell to minus twenty-two degrees Fahrenheit.

Leonov and Belyayev spent two freezing nights in their spacecraft before being rescued. Like other embarrassing, deadly, or near-fatal mishaps in the Soviet space program, the truth of Voskhod 2—and its death-defying crew—was not released for twenty-five years.

Korolev's successful multi-crew-member Voskhod program had given the Russians two more impressive victories. The Soviet Union had beaten America in this round of the space race. But with each two-person Gemini flight, the US was closing the gap.

Project Gemini was designed to help NASA master the skills necessary to reach the moon. Between March 1965 and November 1966, ten Gemini crews flew twelve successful flights. Gemini 4 achieved America's first space walk. For twenty-three minutes, Edward H. White II was tethered outside the Gemini capsule, staring into space through his helmet's gold-plated visor, which protected his eyes from the sun's dangerous rays. White said he was brokenhearted when he was ordered to end the space walk, calling it the "saddest moment of my life." On the Gemini 5 flight, Gordon Cooper and Charles "Pete" Conrad Jr. were the first American astronauts to remain in orbit for more than a week. Gemini 8, with John Glenn and David

Scott aboard, succeeded in connecting with another spacecraft. When Project Gemini concluded on November 15, 1966, in less than two years, America had achieved all of Project Gemini's mission objectives and taken the lead in the space race.

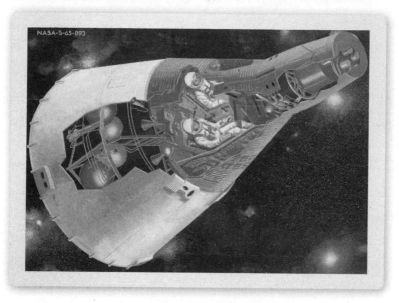

Gemini spacecraft.

• • •

Korolev refused to accept the success of Project Gemini as a defeat. In December 1965, his stubborn campaign to restore funding to the N-1 program was finally successful. He planned to land on the moon by 1968. Given the advanced stages of the Apollo program, succeeding with the N-1 was an enormous challenge.

In Huntsville, von Braun was not without his own worries. The five temperamental F-1 engines needed to boost the Apollo capsule and the Saturn V rocket into space had to pass one more test.

Marshall Space Flight Center

APRIL 16, 1965

HUNTSVILLE, ALABAMA

"Attention, all personnel! Attention, all personnel! Clear the test stand area," a voice boomed through the loudspeaker. All systems were "go" for the first static test firing of all five F-1 engines, which made up the first stage of the Saturn V rocket. The test was two months ahead of its original schedule. The challenge had been creating and then *containing* the explosive alchemy between liquid oxygen and kerosene when the fuel poured into the engine bell at a rate fast enough to fill a family-size swimming pool every ten seconds. The ambitious von Braun knew that a failure at this stage could be a devastating setback. Combustion instability was unpredictable and a persistent concern. But whether it was balancing potentially explosive elements in a rocket engine or balancing his troubling past with his hopes for the future, von Braun never lost his footing. Since his arrival in the US, his life had been an exercise in containing the potentially explosive truth in his pursuit of spaceflight. For two decades, his connection to Mittelwerk had remained hidden.

Years of planning, exhaustive testing, failures, and redesigns had brought von Braun and the temperamental F-1 engine to another defining moment.

The countdown began. "Five, four, three, two, one . . . Ignition!"

With that command, flames boiled from the base of the five F-1 engines in a deafening roar. Windows around Huntsville rattled. The ground rumbled, but there was no sign of combustion instability. Each of the five bell-shaped F-1 engines weighed over nine tons, generated 1.5 million pounds of thrust, and had a potential energy output equal to the power of eighty-five Hoover Dams, more than enough to push Apollo to the moon and reassure Wernher von Braun that the engine, like his troubling past, could be contained.

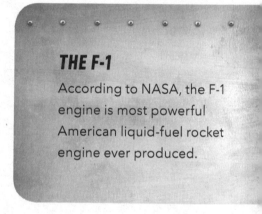

THE F-1

According to NASA, the F-1 engine is most powerful American liquid-fuel rocket engine ever produced.

The enthusiasm surrounding the space race in the US and the USSR concealed a darker reality lurking beneath the high-tech competition. In the years to come, the price paid by some of those working on American and Soviet moon shots would not be calculated on a government budget sheet. The breakneck pace of innovation drove many to early graves. The unseen cost was exacted in long work hours, the unhealthy lifestyle (little sleep, poor eating habits, and lots of cigarette smoking), and broken marriages. The near-constant emotional stress that came with their high-stakes jobs was extraordinary. It wasn't just astronauts and cosmonauts who put it all on the line. Countless people, in the United States and the USSR, whose names were never known, toiled in machine shops, factories, and laboratories, while their families wondered when they would see their loved one at the dinner table again. Political pressure and the all-consuming obsession with winning the space race compelled many to accomplish the near impossible at any price.

For Korolev the cost was deteriorating health. By December 1965, he had been sick for some time, and tired easily. But the bullish chief designer concealed his symptoms from his closest colleagues and friends. His secretary, Antonina Zlotnikova, never suspected her boss was sick and recalled him saying, "I will die right here, at this desk." Korolev's strong-looking physique helped hide the truth, but his heart had been compromised by years of suffering in prison. He wrote to his second wife, Nina, from Baikonur, saying, "I am somehow unusually deeply tired . . . sometimes the little heart aches a bit." When medical tests revealed a bleeding polyp in Korolev's intestine, doctors scheduled surgery for January. The large rocket enterprise could function without him during his recovery, but Korolev's team knew that if the Soviets were going to beat the Americans, it would take every ounce of Korolev's strength and intellect. Sheer force of will was no longer enough to keep his rocket program alive.

Vietnam

As Korolev confronted the reality of his declining health, the Soviet Union and America sank deeper into the Cold War. A controversial jungle conflict in the Southeast Asian country of Vietnam was coming to a head. As with the Korean War in the early 1950s, the two countries took sides against each other in the fight. North Vietnam was supported by the Soviet Union and South Vietnam by the United States. A small number of American military advisers had been present in Vietnam during the 1950s. Beginning in 1961, those numbers increased. By 1965 combat troops had arrived. As the war escalated, young American men were drafted into mandatory military service and sent to fight in Vietnam. For the first time, a war was televised in the United States. Nowadays, life without television and streaming devices seems incomprehensible. In the 1960s, however, television was at-home technology that didn't fit in your pocket. Twenty-four-hour cable news stations did not exist, and the nightly news broadcasts lasted for only fifteen to thirty minutes *per day*. Televisions became more commonplace in American households. For the first time, families could tune in to the evening news and watch film footage as journalists reported from the war zone. Blood that was shed half a world away seeped into American living rooms. Safe from bullets and bombs, Americans witnessed the carnage, death, and misery of battle. Eventually, these gruesome scenes, along with a high number of casualties, outraged many Americans, who believed the war was pointless and impossible to win.

On April 17, 1965, one day after the successful test of the F-1 engines, between 15,000 and 25,000 peaceful protesters descended on Washington, DC, to march against the war in Vietnam. Up to that point, it was the largest peace protest in US history. Americans were asking tough questions of President Lyndon Johnson. Why was the Vietnam War necessary? When would it end? Why was the United States spending billions on a moon shot when teenagers as young as eighteen years of age were being sent to to die in a war that seemed to worsen with each passing day?

Civil rights leaders added their voices to the protest. Reverend Ralph Abernathy, who had marched with Dr. Martin Luther King Jr., criticized Apollo spending. He wanted the government to reallocate the money to solve social problems for the people suffering on planet Earth. Abernathy argued the money should be used to make people's lives better by building houses for the homeless and feeding the hungry.

The space race had revealed a division in American priorities. Should scientific discovery truly take precedence when soldiers were dying in Vietnam and poverty-stricken Americans were going hungry at home? Why would a nation invest vast sums of money in a space race that, in the minds of many, had no practical application in making life better on Earth? Did the race to the moon matter more than a human life?

Perhaps Korolev would have agreed that reaching the moon was worth any sacrifice. He had compromised his health, relinquished his peace of mind, and been forced to work in complete anonymity. Through it all, the chief designer never doubted how much he would give to the endeavor. And maybe one day, if he lived long enough, he would at last hear the voices of his Russian comrades proudly chanting his name in Red Square.

CHAPTER 36

DA SVIDANIYA ("GOODBYE")

While Americans debated the wisdom of funding the moon landing, work on the N-1 rocket proceeded in the Soviet Union. On January 4, 1966, Vasily Mishin, Korolev's deputy of twenty years, held a meeting with key managers of the N-1 moon-landing team. The group didn't expect Korolev to attend because he was scheduled for surgery the next day. When Boris Chertok looked up from the meeting to see Korolev at the door, he noticed that the chief designer wasn't himself. "He was wearing his coat and fur hat . . . and looked at us with a tender and wistful smile." Chertok recalled that he seemed "run-down, melancholy, and lost in his thoughts." The chief designer nodded to the group and said, "Well, carry on!" The engineers said goodbye, and without entering the room, Korolev walked away.

On January 5, 1966, he was readmitted to the hospital for

polyp surgery. The doctors reassured Korolev that there was no real cause for concern, explaining that it was "less complicated than an appendectomy." He was expected to return to work in one week, but that did little to improve the chief designer's foul mood. He didn't like to sit still when there was so much work to do. Now he was stuck in a hospital bed. He was miserable and aggravated by everything, from his misplaced slippers to his poor hearing. (For a relatively young man, not yet sixty years old, Korolev suffered premature hearing loss, possibly caused by the roar of engines at the Baikonur Cosmodrome.) He had a hearing aid, but the hardheaded chief designer refused to use it. As his anxiety peaked, he said to Nina, "I can't work like this any longer."

Korolev left Mishin in charge while he was hospitalized. Although Mishin lacked Korolev's political finesse and influence, he had agreed to serve in the role until Korolev could resume his duties. He trusted that the rugged chief designer would recover, as he always did from these attacks of poor health.

Soon after Korolev's departure, Mishin's authority was challenged when he was severely reprimanded by a senior official. The exact reason is unknown, but the encounter rattled an already overwhelmed Mishin. The stress of the job was too much to bear, and Mishin wanted to quit. Another engineer who worked with Korolev, and knew Mishin was preparing to resign, contacted Korolev in the hospital.

The chief designer knew he could not run his sprawling rocket program from a hospital bed. If there was any hope of continuing against the Americans, Korolev had to convince Mishin to stay until he returned.

Korolev picked up the phone.

"What are you doing?" Korolev asked Mishin, who replied that he was writing a letter of resignation.

"It is hard enough to work with you, but with him," Mishin said, referring to the senior official who had admonished him, "there is no way." Korolev held firm and told Mishin to tear up the letter. "Ministers come and ministers go, but we stay in our own business." A few well-chosen words from his longtime leader had convinced Mishin to stay.

Korolev went into surgery at eight a.m., on Friday, January 14, 1966. It was supposed to be a relatively short procedure, but as Korolev's daughter, Natalia, later described it, the operation did not go according to plan. "My father hemorrhaged on the operating table." The surgeon "cut the abdomen to stop the bleeding, and found a cancerous tumor, which had not been visible before." According to a nurse present in the operating room, the tumor was the size of two fists. For eight hours, Korolev was under anesthesia. He survived the operation, but his prognosis was grim. The surgeon closed him up with the knowledge that once he regained consciousness, the chief designer only had a few months left to live. His team at the OKB-1 workshop would be devastated to learn that the chief designer was dying. He had hidden his declining health for years. Korolev's team couldn't have known that his condition was life-threatening, or that he might not live long enough to see his N-1 rocket launched to the moon.

But Korolev wouldn't be granted those last few months of life. Thirty minutes after surgery, he stopped breathing. Doctors raced back to Korolev's room, but it was too late. His battered heart, damaged from years of abuse in the Gulag, could not sustain him.

At age fifty-nine, Sergei Korolev, the Soviet Union's hidden hero of the space race, was dead.

On January 16, *Pravda*, the Soviet newspaper, announced publicly, for the first time, the long-held secret identity of chief designer Sergei Pavlovich Korolev. Leonid Brezhnev, who had replaced Nikita Khrushchev as the new Soviet premier in 1964, decided that the chief designer's name could finally be revealed. His obituary was published along with his photograph. The once-invisible man materialized before the world.

His longtime associate and fellow engineer Boris Chertok was given just one hour to draft the obituary and put Korolev's legacy into words. When Chertok submitted his draft to Ivan Dmitriyevich Serbin, head of the Central Committee's Department of the Defense Industry, for approval, Serbin said, "It can't be this modest." Chertok took the opportunity to insert another line, one that he felt encapsulated Korolev's strength of character in overcoming repression under Stalin's rule. He wrote: "Korolev remained an ardent patriot and steadfastly pursed his goal—to fulfill the dream of spaceflight, despite years of unjust persecution."

Chertok had taken care in choosing those words, but he had gone too far by hinting that Korolev had been victimized by Stalin's purges. "I was attempting to inform the reader that [Korolev] had suffered repression," Chertok wrote in his memoir. He wanted to reflect Korolev's tenacious spirit; that the chief designer had survived and thrived for a time in spite of all that he'd suffered. Korolev had endured the Great Terror and a six-year-long prison nightmare as an innocent man, but there would be no public mention of the catastrophic role Stalin had played in Korolev's life. Chertok watched as "Serbin frowned, and without saying a word, firmly crossed out those lines." Stalin's reign of terror still loomed over those who remembered.

Brezhnev announced plans for a full state funeral in Red Square. The Russian people would have the opportunity to pay their respects at a public viewing at noon the next day in the House of Unions. By nine a.m., a line had already formed in the bitter cold, with the first person waiting three hours to enter.

Thousands more Soviet citizens descended on the capital to pay their respects to their comrade. Boris Chertok understood why. "A particle of truth had finally been revealed to them," he wrote. "There was a general sense of being party to a partially divulged secret." Finally, the Russian people could see who had brought such glory to the homeland by snatching repeated victories away from the Americans. "There was a shared grief and a shared pride. It was late in coming, but the people had been given the opportunity to pay tribute to the great Korolev. . . . It was as if everyone who passed by his casket brushed up against these historic achievements." Cosmonauts, and many of the Soviet space program's other chief designers and deputies, served as an honor guard at Korolev's casket. They stood in shifts, trading places with one another in a final show of respect and devotion. "We wanted to be with Korolev a little longer, even though he was no longer with us," Chertok wrote.

Korolev was cremated, and the following day his ashes were interred in the wall of the Kremlin alongside those of past Soviet leaders and heroes. It was a historic public honor for a man who had once been branded a traitor but had risen above every inconceivable obstacle to lead his country in the space race. Now it would fall to his trusted deputy, Vasily Mishin, to carry on what Korolev had started, as the new leader of Korolev's rocket team.

Russians pay their final respects at Sergei Korolev's funeral.

In America, von Braun finally learned the identity of his brilliant rival. Sergei Korolev was the worthy adversary who had driven him—and the world—into the space race. He knew Korolev's death was a crushing blow to the Russians. Would they ever make it to the moon without him?

CHAPTER 37

"A ROUGH ROAD LEADS TO THE STARS"

While the Soviets reeled from Korolev's death, the American space program had its own setbacks with three years remaining in President Kennedy's countdown. The Saturn V rocket still wasn't ready, so it was decided that upcoming Apollo test flight missions would launch with the Saturn I rocket, an earlier model. The tests were designed to confirm procedures to save lives by anticipating problems, but there were no guarantees. Astronaut Gus Grissom, who had once been asked about the possibility of dying in the quest for the moon, said, "If we die, we want people to accept it. We're in a risky business, and we hope that if anything happens to us it will not delay the program. The conquest of space is worth the risk of life."

On January 27, 1967, an Apollo 1 capsule sat on the launchpad at Cape Canaveral. Sealed inside the command module that day were astronauts Roger Chaffee, Gus Grissom, and Edward "Ed" White. The team was conducting a detailed simulation during which the rocket would remain on the pad and not actually launch. During the exercise, the spacecraft disengaged from all its cables and tethers to prove its internal power system was functioning. If all went according to plan during this "plugs out" test, the first actual launch of an Apollo flight would happen one month later.

Left to right: Gus Grissom, Ed White, and Roger Chaffee.

At 5:40 p.m., a communications failure delayed the countdown. At 6:30 p.m., Grissom said, "How are we going to get to the moon if we can't talk between three buildings?" One minute later, a power surge was recorded. Soon after, White could be heard:

"We've got a fire in the cockpit!"

The capsule's oxygen had ignited. All three astronauts were trapped. Getting them out of the capsule immediately was impossible. Under normal conditions the hatch took ninety seconds to open. Due to the tremendous heat generated by the fire, technicians struggled for five minutes before finally opening it. By then, all three astronauts were dead.

It was NASA's first catastrophic accident. The American people were shocked and saddened by the deaths of Chaffee, White, and Grissom. Each of the three astronauts was honored with a military funeral in accordance with their branches of service. While the country mourned, the incident raised troubling questions about safety, endangering the fledgling space program. If something like this could happen in a rocket that wasn't leaving the ground, how could the safety of any astronaut ever be guaranteed? It couldn't, and the Apollo 1 astronauts had willingly accepted that risk.

An investigation of the fire began immediately and lasted eighteen months, delaying the Apollo program while the command module was completely redesigned. The cause of the fatal blaze was a short circuit in a wire bundle near Grissom's seat. A spark had ignited the flammable material inside the capsule's oxygen-rich environment. New safety features were implemented to prevent future fire hazards. Among other modifications, the flammable material was replaced and a new hatch installed that opened outward and more quickly. Chaffee, White, and Grissom had made the ultimate sacrifice for their country, and their deaths served as a chilling reminder of the risks undertaken in attempting to reach the moon. Von Braun later said that America had lost "three good friends and valiant pioneers," whose deaths reminded him of the Latin saying *ad astra per aspera*—a rough road leads to the stars.[12]

Soyuz 1: First Flight

Three months after the Apollo 1 tragedy in America, on a bright, sunlit morning, a Soviet helicopter zoomed across the Kazakhstan desert, searching for the landing site of cosmonaut Vladimir Komarov and his Soyuz 1 space capsule. Komarov, who had been a crewmember of the risky and overcrowded three-person Voskhod mission, had a new spacecraft all to himself on a solo flight.

The innovative Soyuz rocket and space capsule, under development at the time of Korolev's death, were destined to become the future of spaceflight for the Russians. At the time of Komarov's flight, the capsule and its launch vehicle—a rocket based on the R-7 Semyorka—remained unproven.

It had been two years since the Soviets had launched a crewed flight, with cosmonauts Leonov and Belyayev achieving the world's first space walk. Sergei Korolev had been dead more than a year. Despite the delays caused by the Apollo 1 accident, the

---

12   *Ad astra per aspera* is commonly translated as "Through hardship to the stars." A plaque honoring the Apollo 1 crew was later placed at Launch Complex 34, where Chaffee, White, and Grissom perished. It is inscribed with von Braun's slightly altered translation, "A rough road leads to the stars."

United States' space program was advancing much faster than the Soviets'. The big Saturn V was almost ready, and the Soviets had yet to perfect a rocket that could compete with it. Vasily Mishin hoped that the Soyuz 1 flight would succeed and reassert his country's position in the space race.

After a picture-perfect launch on April 24, a series of failures in the Soyuz 1 power system complicated the flight. The capsule relied on both fuel and solar energy to function. First, the left solar panel failed to deploy, robbing the spacecraft of a power source. This also created an imbalance in the capsule, which prevented the functioning solar panel from turning toward the sun. If Komarov was unable to solve these problems, the Soyuz 1 could be thrust into a higher orbit or reenter Earth's atmosphere at the wrong angle, burning up during descent.

Engineers on the ground calculated that Soyuz 1 had enough fuel for nineteen orbits—about one day. They wanted Komarov to head home by the seventeenth orbit. That would give the cosmonaut two more orbits as a buffer. After that, it would be too late.

Due to the capsule's loss of power, Komarov would have to manually steer the Soyuz for reentry into Earth's atmosphere—a maneuver that he had never simulated in training. The commands were transmitted to Komarov; he executed them as instructed and began deorbiting. Communications between Komarov and ground control were sporadic, but the cosmonaut sounded composed. When ground control received the signal that the capsule had landed, a helicopter was dispatched to rendezvous with the Soyuz 1 on the ground. It was almost six thirty a.m.

Inside the chopper, officials scanned the Kazakhstan desert for a sign of Komarov and his spacecraft. Suddenly the helicopter pilot made a steep right turn and steered toward the ground. The capsule came into view. It was resting on its side, engulfed in smoke and fire. Witnesses reported seeing the capsule's failed parachute, meant to slow its descent, flapping uselessly behind the Soyuz 1. Komarov had hit the ground traveling 115–130 feet per second and died on impact.

The Soviets did not try to hide Komarov's death, because cosmonauts were recognizable public figures and their missions were heavily publicized propaganda events. However, the details of Komarov's flight, in keeping with the Soviet tradition of secrecy, were classified for decades. In a show of solidarity, American astronauts sent condolences to the Soviet Union via telegram. "We are very saddened by the loss of Col. Komarov," they wrote in part. "We particularly want to express our deep sense of sympathy to Mrs. Komarov, their children and his fellow cosmonauts." Both space programs had suffered terrible losses on their rough road to the stars.

The following year, 1968, delivered another devastating loss to the Soviet Union and the already heartbroken Russian people: on March 27, Yuri Gagarin was killed when his MiG-15 fighter jet crashed outside Moscow. For years, rumors have persisted that Gagarin's death was deliberate. His fellow cosmonuat, Alexei Leonov, maintained that the crash was an accident.

After launching Sputnik, the Soviets had dominated the early years of the competition. Now they were barely keeping their heads above water. But in death Korolev had one card left to play: the N-1.

Throughout the mid-1960s, CIA spy satellites regularly photographed the Soviet Union. As intelligence analysts reviewed reconnaissance images, they spotted what appeared to be new construction. The Russians appeared to be building at least two new launch towers. Judging by their size, the Soviets had engineered another huge rocket. Were they attempting a moon shot? If the first flag to be planted on the moon was going to be American, NASA needed to pick up the pace.

CHAPTER 38

APOLLO TAKES FLIGHT

George Mueller, NASA associate administrator for manned space flight—and one of von Braun's bosses—had a radical idea about how to accelerate the Apollo schedule. He wanted to streamline production of the Saturn V by changing the way the rocket was tested. Mueller proposed an uncrewed "all-up" test as the very first test of the giant Saturn V. The rocket, with both its command module and service modules, would be launched on a flight path that would simulate a return from the moon.

He had first suggested the idea in 1964 during a visit to Huntsville. At the time, the meticulous German rocketeers had dismissed Mueller's idea as reckless. They had their own tried-and-true method: testing the rocket stages individually, adding each new stage after the previous one had been proven sound. By 1967, however, the all-up test strategy looked more appealing. After the deaths of Grissom, Chaffee, and White, the Apollo capsule had to be completely redesigned, delaying the Apollo program. If Mueller's plan succeeded, it would save time by eliminating unnecssary test flights. The convincing argument, coupled with fear that the Soviets would launch their own moon rocket first, changed von Braun's mind.

The uncrewed Apollo 4 mission would be the first-ever Saturn V to launch from Cape Kennedy, Florida.[13]

Apollo 4: "All Up"

On November 9, 1967, the F-1 engines screamed to life beneath Apollo 4, with a force that shook the walls of the Launch Control Center three miles away. Inside, plaster rained down on news reporter Walter Cronkite as he covered the televised launch for the CBS network. Cronkite and a colleague held the glass window behind them, fearing it would break. The vibrations triggered earthquake seismometers. Someone later remarked that "the question was not whether the Saturn V had risen, but whether Florida had sunk." Veteran NASA contractor Jim Jenkins, who worked with the Apollo program, remembered fifty-two years later the deafening roar of the Saturn V engines. "When that thing fired," he said, "it sounded like God himself was clearing his throat." The successful launch of Apollo 4 in Mueller's all-up test cleared the way for two more successful uncrewed test flights, Apollo 5 and Apollo 6. The next

---

13 NASA altered its naming system after Apollo 1. The sequence of Apollo missions skips from Apollo 1 to Apollo 4.

mission would be the first flight with astronauts since the deaths of astronauts Chaffee, White, and Grissom aboard Apollo 1.

Apollo 7: The First NASA Crew in Space

On October 11, 1968, Apollo 7 was on the pad. NASA was encouraged that Kennedy's deadline could still be met. Now it was up to astronauts Walter "Wally" Schirra, Donn F. Eisele, and Walter Cunningham to prove that the redesigned command module was sound. At ignition, the Saturn I rocket lifted into the sky without incident.

As they orbited the Earth, all three astronauts came down with the world's first space colds. Sick days weren't an option for astronauts who were whirring around the planet at thousands of miles per hour. Apollo 7's ten-day to-do list included separating the command and service modules, turning the spacecraft around, and simulating docking. The ailing astronauts did not fare as well as their spacecraft during the mission—they learned that blowing one's nose in outer space was painful, as fluids don't drain easily in zero gravity.

On day three, the crew conducted the first-ever live television broadcast from space and held up signs with handwritten messages written on them. Commander Schirra's read, *Keep those cards and letters coming in, folks.*

At reentry, after almost eleven days in space and still sick, the astronauts refused to wear their helmets as they returned to Earth. They needed to be able to reach their faces to blow their noses during descent. Otherwise, the resulting pressure could burst their eardrums.

On October 22, they splashed down safely, having successfully orbited the Earth 163 times. Their mission complete, the Apollo 7 astronauts prepared to watch as the next crew took their positions on the launchpad forty days later.

Apollo 8: "Round the Moon and Back"

DECEMBER 21–27, 1968

Astronauts James A. Lovell, Frank Borman, and William A. Anders would not be home for the holidays in 1968. Instead, they were aboard the Apollo 8 capsule, as the first crewed mission to be carried into space by the Saturn V and the first to orbit the moon. "Everyone was motivated. Everyone was dedicated," Apollo 8 commander Frank Borman said. "The basic idea was to beat the Russians to the moon. . . . We were determined to meet it—to beat it."

Their flight path carried them on a six-day trip from Earth, around the moon and back. Their mission goals included testing navigation procedures, communications, and photographing the lunar surface. Future Apollo missions would need this information to land. Years later, astronaut James Lovell recalled the feeling of looking down at the moon from their capsule: "We were like school kids looking through a candy store window, staring at the unnamed craters as they slowly passed us by."

During the flight's fourth orbit around the moon, Borman

spotted an object outside the spacecraft that forever changed the way humanity would see itself. "Suddenly I looked out the window and here was this gorgeous orb coming up and I thought holy moly," Borman recalled. It was the Earth; a lush blue-white-and-green-swirled marble suspended in the complete blackness of the universe. "Oh, my God! Look at that picture over there! Here's the Earth coming up. Wow, is that pretty!" Anders said as he snapped a picture through the window of the capsule.

No human being had ever seen the planet from this perspective. As Anders continued to snap dozens of pictures, the astronauts stared in wonder. They were hundreds of thousands of miles from everything and everyone they knew, risking their lives in the name of exploration. "The vast loneliness is awe-inspiring and it makes you realize just what you have back there on Earth," Lovell said. The photograph, later named *Earthrise*, became the most famous photograph ever taken in space. The image marked the beginning of the environmental movement. For the first time, people could see how fragile the Earth looked in the emptiness of space. It had to be protected. It was home.

The Apollo 8 crew, humbled by their new experience, found it difficult to keep the emotion from their voices as they transmitted a tender message home to Earth that Christmas Eve: "From the crew of the Apollo 8 we close with good night, good luck, a merry Christmas, and God bless all of you—all of you on the good Earth."

It was a moment of profound hope and inspiration in a year that

Earthrise, as first viewed and photographed by the crew of Apollo 8.

had otherwise been, as Jim Lovell later recalled, "disastrous." Back home, America remained at war in Vietnam.

Earlier that year, the Reverend Martin Luther King Jr. and President John F. Kennedy's younger brother, Senator Robert Kennedy, had been assassinated. "To end the year by going around the moon on Christmas Eve," Lovell said, "everything just fell into place."

Apollo 9

MARCH 3, 1969

Two more successful Apollo missions followed the inspiring flight of Apollo 8. The Apollo 9 astronauts, Russell "Rusty" Schweickart, James McDivitt, and David Scott, tested both the command module and the lunar module components. While piloting them in orbit, they practiced firing the engine to bring the two modules back together. The difficult maneuver proved all the hardware was sound. Schweickart and Scott performed simultaneous EVAs (extravehicular activities), or space walks. Ten days later, Apollo 9 splashed down safely. One last test mission remained before Apollo 11 would attempt to land on the moon.

Apollo 10: Nine Miles from the Moon

MAY 18–26, 1969

The mission facing the crew of Apollo 10 astronauts Eugene Cernan, Thomas P. Stafford, and John W. Young was nothing less than the greatest dress rehearsal of the Apollo program. For the first time, the lunar module would separate from the command module to make its way toward the moon with Cernan and Stafford aboard. Young would stay behind to helm the command module.

Cernan and Stafford flew within 47,000 feet of the moon's surface, testing landing radar and recording observations of possible Apollo 11 touchdown sites. The crew did everything but land on the moon.

"What a place!" Cernan reported to ground control as their spacecraft swept over the lunar surface. "You know, it almost looks like this is a painting."

The flight nearly ended in disaster as procedures were under way to redock with the command module. As the lunar module's engine fired, the moon's horizon spun past their window six times. Their ship was spinning out of control. "I heard the thrusters start to fire," Stafford remembered. "I heard this ba-bang, bang, bang." His pilot's instincts took over. Stafford hit the staging switch and went to a hard stop. With quick thinking and steady nerves, the danger passed as quickly as it came. The team re-docked with the command module. "We were fighter pilots, test pilots, so we knew what the risks were and you did everything you could to mitigate the risk. But there was a risk. We understood that," Stafford said.

Apollo 10 was a record-setting flight, returning to Earth in forty-two hours, at a speed of 24,791 miles per hour, the fastest speed attained by a human vehicle.

The Apollo 10 astronauts debriefed the Apollo 11 crew on their findings. "We had all the procedures worked out . . . down to the last fifty thousand feet," Stafford remembered. The Apollo 11 crew would have to take it from there.

Following the deaths of the Apollo 1 astronauts, the well-documented test flights that followed went down in history books as huge successes in the American space program. The United States had overcome the tragedy and continued on the road to the stars.

Unbeknownst to the United States, the Russians watched the Apollo test flights with grim resignation. The Americans were leaving them in the dust of the Kazakhstan desert. Apollo 8 was a three-part defeat for the Soviet space program: the first-ever successful flight around the moon, the public reaction to the *Earthrise* photo, and the astronauts' heartfelt message delivered from space on Christmas Eve. It was a stunning victory of both science *and* propaganda. Everything was falling into place for von Braun and NASA. Korolev's towering N-1 rocket was the Soviets' last hope.

Korolev's Moon Shot

By the time the N-1 was stacked on the Baikonur launchpad for its first uncrewed flight in February 1969, the chief designer had been dead for three years. Korolev's moon rocket steamed and hissed in the cold Kazakhstan air. Vasily Mishin's crews had been working twenty-four-hour shifts to prepare the rocket for launch. There had been no money to build expensive test stands. They would know if the rocket worked when it launched.

At ignition, the N-1's thirty-engine cluster fired and the rocket began to

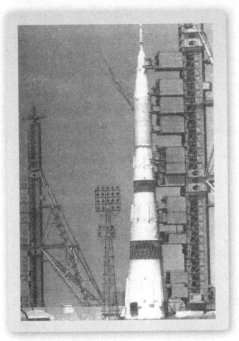

A mockup of the N-1 rocket at Baikonur, 1967.

rise, along with the morale of the exhausted Soviet engineering team. "In those first few moments there was a sort of uplifting feeling. Yes! It's taken off! Yes! It hasn't blown up on the spot! This was already a great victory," engineer Boris Chertok recalled. But the rocket exploded one minute into the flight. It was later determined that a small piece of metal had been sucked into one of the rocket's engines, causing it to malfunction. In the incident report, the Soviets adhered to their strict policy of secrecy when it came to mistakes and accidents. The result was a feeble and almost comical understatement of the accident's true cause. The report's author wrote that the engine was "sensitive to incoming foreign objects."

On July 3, 1969, another N-1 lifted off from Baikonur. The rocket rose briefly before collapsing and exploding with the equivalent energy of a nuclear bomb—the largest rocket explosion in history. The debris field spanned six miles.

Without Korolev, the once-great Soviet space program had crumbled. Rather than admit or acknowledge their failure in the space race at the time, the truth of the top secret N-1 moon program and its failures remained classified from the Russian people. Participants in the program were forbidden to speak about their involvement. It wasn't until 1989, near the collapse of the Soviet Union, that the country learned it had tried—and failed—to build a rocket that would land on the moon. Vasily Mishin finally broke his silence about his pivotal role in the doomed N-1 project. In 1990, he wrote: "Only he who does nothing makes mistakes. We, the successors of S. P. Korolev, did everything we could, but our efforts proved to be inadequate."

CHAPTER 39

"ONE SMALL STEP"

On July 20, 1969, seventeen days after the second failed N-1 rocket launch in the Soviet Union, Von Braun prepared to watch as his lifelong dream of space travel came true. America was about to attempt the world's first moon landing. It was the realization of Wernher von Braun's boyhood vision of building a spaceship. He had doodled its likeness in a school notebook. To secure funding for his rocket research, he had agreed to join the Nazi Party and become an officer in Hitler's SS. As his critics would later argue, this dream was von Braun's justification for turning a blind eye to the atrocities at the Nazis' Mittelwerk V-2 factory. It was the reason he risked his life by betraying the Nazis to surrender to the United States at the end of World War II. During those early, dry Fort Bliss years, it had been his sustaining hope, before the US government opened its mind—and its wallet—to the possibilities of spaceflight. In exchange for his expertise and the V-2 technology, his status as a Nazi officer had been buried within classified documents. Every choice he had made had led to this moment, when his rocket would send humankind to the moon. Twenty-four years after arriving in the United States, Wernher von Braun was considered by many to be an American hero.

Apollo 11 lifted off on July 16. Four days later, on the morning of the moon landing, NASA guidance officer (GUIDO) Steve Bales arrived in the Apollo Mission Control Center in Houston, an hour early. The dark-haired, blue-eyed twenty-six year-old's job was to "monitor the lunar module's guidance computer," he said. It was an unlikely career path for the son of a janitor and hairstylist from the small town of Fremont, Iowa, with a population of less than five hundred people. Bales's life had changed at age thirteen when he turned on his family's television set and watched a Walt Disney "Tomorrowland" episode starring Wernher von Braun. The show, Bales said, "probably more than anything else, influenced me to study aerospace engineering."

At his workstation, Bales lit a cigarette and began reviewing his notes. When the first cigarette burned to its filter, he lit another. It was a stressful job, and almost everyone in Mission Control smoked. In those days, warnings about the dangers of cigarettes were often ignored. The only thing thicker than the haze of smoke in Mission Control was the tension. Bales remembered feeling like he could "cut it with a knife." He didn't know it then, but eight hours later, the lives of the astronauts would be in his hands.

Apollo 11

"Program alarm." The calm voice of Commander Neil Armstrong sounded inside NASA ground control. Half a billion people world-wide waited as astronauts Neil Armstrong and Edwin "Buzz" Aldrin, in the lunar module (also known as "Eagle"), journeyed toward the moon. Fellow astronaut Michael Collins orbited above them in the Columbia command module. The astronauts were four minutes into the landing sequence and 33,000 feet from the lunar surface.

"It's a 1202," Armstrong said. Neither he nor Aldrin knew how to interpret the computer screen displaying error code "1202," and there wasn't much time.

Everyone in Mission Control, including von Braun, waited for Bales to make a decision. Guidance officers were trained to respond in an instant to situations like this. What Bales said next would determine whether Armstrong and Aldrin continued their flight or aborted the historic mission.

He searched his memory. The astronauts were racing toward the moon. The window of time in which they could initiate a safe and successful abort was closing. Worse, no one knew if an abort was actually possible. The Eagle could crash into the lunar surface. Some 240,000 miles away from Earth, the lives of the astronauts depended on Bales's response.

Suddenly the voice of another guidance specialist, twenty-four-year-old Jack Garman, burst into his headset. "Steve! It's on our little list!" Then Bales remembered. Gene Kranz, the Apollo flight director, had ordered each guidance specialist to write down every error code that the mission could encounter and tape the list to his desk.

A 1202 meant the computer was overloaded with information. The alarm signaled that it was sorting too much data at once. As long as the alarm was intermittent, the landing could proceed. If the alarm became sustained, they would be forced to abort. Bales knew what to do.

Seconds had passed since Armstrong's request for a reading.

"We're GO on that alarm," Bales said confidently into his headset's microphone.

The capsule communicator (CAPCOM) relayed the message to Armstrong.

"Roger," Armstrong replied.

Armstrong and Aldrin weren't out of the woods yet. The Eagle was off course and they had overshot their original landing coordinates. The predetermined site had been ideal, with a smooth surface free of debris, but the field before Commander Armstrong now was a deep crater, littered with large moon-rock boulders. There was nowhere to land and they were running out of fuel.

Armstrong, a skilled fighter pilot, held his nerve as he continued to steer the spacecraft in search of a safe spot to set it down.

The landing sequence reached the sixty-second mark, and precious fuel reserves plummeted. "Better remind them there ain't no damn gas stations on the moon," Kranz said.

At the thirty-second mark, the Eagle was less than ten feet from the surface. Moon dust swirled beneath it, and a new alert appeared on Armstrong's lunar module console.

CONTACT LIGHT.

Armstrong's voice returned to the ground control room: "Houston, Tranquility Base here. The Eagle has landed."

Later, as Armstrong exited the capsule and climbed down its ladder, von Braun watched from Mission Control with tears in his eyes, seeing his life's work culminate on a television monitor. "That's one small step for man," Armstrong said as his foot touched the surface of the moon, "one giant leap for mankind."

Half a world away, inside a Soviet military base control room, cosmonaut Alexei Leonov, who had crossed his fingers in a gesture of hope for Armstrong and Aldrin, burst into cheers as the historic moment unfolded on a television screen in front of him: "I swear to God . . . we hoped the guys would make it. We wanted this to happen." The Soviet leadership sent a congratulatory letter to the United States, but they did not issue a public comment. The Soviet newspaper *Pravda* allotted two paragraphs to the moon-landing story, placing it at the bottom of an interior page. Only select government officials were permitted to view actual video footage of America's victory in the space race.

Millions of people worldwide had gathered around radios or television sets that day, waiting for updates. They cried and cheered for what they were seeing and hearing but could scarcely comprehend: in a grainy black-and-white video, Armstrong and Aldrin were planting an American flag on the moon. Classrooms and living rooms around the world erupted into applause. In the coming weeks and years, thousands of letters from enthusiastic people around the world poured in, congratulating NASA and the Apollo 11 astronauts for their unprecedented achievement.

From Blacon, England, thirteen-year-old Michael Jennings and his mother, Margaret, wrote: "The night of the landing, we didn't go to bed at all . . . we were with you every minute." Eleven-year-old André von Hebra in São Paulo, Brazil, had found a career path: "I adore space and everything which is connected with it. . . . When I am grown up, I will be an astronaut." For ten-year-old Marianne Malden, who was living in Okinawa, Japan, with her missionary parents, it had been a long night. "My parents had to pour cold water on my face to keep me awake but I saw it and I'll never forget it." The same went for Jerry Hammond of Glens Falls, New York, who shared that he, too, had sacrificed sleep, staying awake for thirty-eight straight hours "to record all of the news of [the] flight." But Hammond's motivation for watching the event's media coverage was grief. "My only son was killed in Vietnam in October 1968," he wrote. "And my interest in your flight was the only thing that kept me from really breaking up."

Von Braun's emotions must have been overwhelming as he watched the flag of his adopted country stake its claim on the moon.

He had been obsessed by the idea of a moon landing for as long as he could remember. He was so convinced he could make it possible that perhaps in some way it also felt inevitable. Von Braun had kept his word to himself and to the American people, to whom he had tirelessly evangelized about the promise of exploration. He helped inspire the creation of the space program and courted the admiration of influential people in his lifelong quest. Wernher von Braun was an engineer and a brilliant manager of people. At heart, he was also a dreamer so obsessed with the realization of his dream that he had been willing to do whatever was necessary to make it come true. What was it that made him able to confront the possibility of failure on such a grand scale, without allowing anything to stop him? Whatever it was—confidence, determination, hubris, or brazen self-interest—it defined his character and choices and made the moon landing possible.

CHAPTER 40

RETURN TO ROCKET CITY

On July 24, 1969, von Braun's Apollo 11 victory came full circle when Armstrong, Aldrin, and Collins safely splashed down in the Pacific Ocean. In Huntsville, city leaders prepared to celebrate its famous rocket engineer and favorite adopted son.

Von Braun's hometown welcome was almost as well choreographed as a rocket launch. Town leadership wanted to capitalize on Huntsville's role in the moon landing. It was an irresistible opportunity to attract national publicity for Huntsville and the Marshall Space Flight Center, with its connection to a world-changing moment. The city was on the cutting edge of the new future in space. Its leaders wanted other technology companies and industries to know that Huntsville welcomed more high-tech businesses to continue building on the foundation laid by von Braun and his team.

In the twenty years since the Germans had arrived at Redstone

Arsenal, the once-rural town had undergone a renaissance. As their work evolved, so did Huntsville, with rocket technology, infrastructure, and aerospace jobs. If the United States owed von Braun a debt of gratitude for winning the space race and masterminding the moon landing, it was fair to say that Huntsville owed him a debt of gratitude as well. The sleepy Watercress Capital of the World emerged as the "Space Capital of the Universe." When the Germans arrived, the city's population had been around 15,000. By 1969 it was over 137,000.

The day of the Apollo 11 splashdown, televised public service announcements invited Huntsvillians to a celebration. Dr. von Braun would be honored with a parade and would give a speech on the city's courthouse steps.

Von Braun was hoisted onto the shoulders of proud civic leaders and carried thorugh the street, as the city of Huntsville celebrated the successful splashdown of Apollo 11 in 1969.

Over five thousand residents and community leaders gathered at the Madison County Courthouse to greet von Braun. He arrived in the time-honored tradition of returning hometown American heroes—seated on the back of a convertible, waving at the enthusiastic crowd. When he stepped out of the car, civic leaders hoisted him onto their shoulders, carrying him to the courthouse and up the steps. Von Braun laughed and continued to wave to the assembled townspeople, who crowded the streets and sidewalks. A local marching band played a triumphant chorus of "Hail to the Chief" as he took his place behind the podium. "That ride was as thrilling as a Saturn V boost into space," he quipped.

Two hours late, von Braun begged forgiveness from the admiring audience, explaining that he had been following the splashdown of the Apollo 11 capsule from his office. His familiar charm was on display, as was his easy smile. When he spoke, it was about the future.

He told the crowd that he was optimistic about an eventual trip to Mars and a space station, speaking in familiar themes of hope and progress. To Huntsville, a city that had been redefined by his work, it sounded like more good things were yet to come. "Now that man has left his planetary cradle and is not confined to Earth," von Braun said, "we must hope that their trip was not in vain. Exploration must continue."

In fact, the Apollo moon-landing program was just getting started. The second successful mission (Apollo 12) lifted off on

November 14, 1969, with astronauts Pete Conrad, Richard Gordon, and Alan Bean aboard. Their historic moon mission was highlighted by the first use of an automatic guidance system that minimized manual control of the craft by the pilot. Other mission goals included developing capabilities to work in the lunar environment and gathering seventy-five pounds of moon rock. The flight also achieved an unscheduled objective: NASA's first documented incident of an off-planet dance performance. Apparently, astronaut Pete Conrad thought his space boots were also dancing shoes and found his zero-gravity groove, dancing on the moon. The astronauts safely returned to Earth ten days later. NASA was riding high on the success of the Apollo program, But the next mission would remind the world just how unpredictable—and dangerous—spaceflight could be.

On April 14, 1970, Apollo 13 commander Jim Lovell spoke six of the most famous words in spaceflight history: "Houston, we've had a problem here."[14] From Apollo 13's command module, Lovell signaled to Mission Control that the spacecraft carrying himself and fellow astronauts Fred Haise and Jack Swigert was in trouble. The crew had been in space for three days when oxygen tank number one had exploded, causing a failure in oxygen tank number two. The potentially deadly onboard explosion forced an abort of their scheduled moon landing and endangered the astronauts. The failing

---

14 Lovell's iconic phrase is frequently misquoted as "Houston, we have a problem."

command module was rapidly losing power. The crew abandoned their ship and moved into the lunar module, which would serve as a lifeboat. But the lunar module wasn't built to transport three astronauts back to Earth and had no mechanism to scrub carbon dioxide from the air. The command module, which was supposed to be their ride home, came equipped with special canisters for this purpose, but they didn't fit in the lunar module "lifeboat." Without them, CO_2 would rise to fatal levels. Engineers on the ground rushed to figure out how to rig an adapter that would make the canisters fit using only items that the astronauts had access to in the lunar module. The resulting contraption was a combination of duct tape, tube socks, and space-suit hoses. It wasn't sophisticated, but it saved their lives, and all three astronauts returned safely to Earth.

NASA would launch four more Apollo missions (14 through 17) to investigate larger areas of the moon's surface and collect samples. Nuclear-powered scientific instruments were also positioned on the moon, and they transmitted data back to Earth for years. Famous video recordings from those subsequent missions show astronauts aboard their lunar roving vehicle, trundling for miles across the surface as they maneuvered around rocks, collecting samples and kicking up moon dust.

CHAPTER 41

LIFE AFTER APOLLO

The last flight in the series would be Apollo 17, in December 1972. It splashed down in a world that was beginning to care less and less about moon shots. America's appetite for space travel had been satisfied and the Russians defeated. The enthusiasm for space exploration that Kennedy had inspired during his unfinished presidency was slipping away with the passage of time. In its place, the urgency of serious problems on Earth took precedence. The jungle war persisted in Vietnam, as well as the ongoing fight for civil rights in the United States. These issues continued to raise justifiable questions from the American people about the wisdom of funneling billions into the space program.

In 1970, von Braun accepted a job in Washington, DC, as deputy associate administrator at NASA. His role was to help the agency plan for the future of space travel. A Mars mission was still on the table, as well as a future space station, but rousing the support and funding would be much more difficult than it had been when Kennedy announced the Apollo program. The agency was betting that von Braun's talents of persuasion would be enough to keep big NASA projects alive.

The news of von Braun's departure was a devastating blow to the people of Huntsville. Although he was a hero to millions around the world, he was a neighbor and an enduring source of civic pride for his community. It was a small comfort that he was not leaving NASA for good, but von Braun's adopted hometown wasn't releasing him without a proper goodbye and a reminder that as far as they were concerned, his departure was temporary.

The banner behind the podium where von Braun would deliver his farewell remarks made this sentiment clear:

DR. WERNHER VON BRAUN: HUNTSVILLE'S FIRST CITIZEN... ON LOAN TO WASHINGTON, DC

The somber feelings of many in attendance were matched by the day's gray skies and rainfall. It was February 24, 1970, officially designated "Wernher von Braun Day." While folks in Huntsville hoped von Braun's stay in Washington was a temporary arrangement, they commemorated his contributions with two lasting symbols of gratitude and affection. The first was a monument dedicated in his honor. The inscription read in part: *Dr. von Braun, whose vision and knowledge made possible the landing of the first man on the moon by the United States, contributed significantly to the life of this community. He will forever be respected and admired by his local fellow citizens.* The second tribute honored von Braun's cultural contribution to the city of Huntsville. He and members of his German engineering team were talented instrumentalists. In the mid-1950s, they had partnered with local musicans to found the Huntsville Symphony Orchestra. The city was planning to build a new fifteen-million-dollar cultural, entertainment, and convention complex and would name it the Von Braun Civic Center.

When he addressed the assembled crowd, von Braun's remarks also contained a warning about the new and challenging obstacles in the future of spaceflight: "My friends, there was dancing in the streets of Huntsville when our first satellite orbited the Earth. There was dancing again when the first Americans landed on the moon. There is only one moon. I'm afraid we can't offer any such spectaculars like that for some years to come. But I'd like to ask you, don't hang up your dancing slippers." Von Braun did not share his conflicted feelings about going to Washington and leaving his old rocket team behind. Instead, he told them that he had enjoyed some of the best years of his life in Alabama.

NASA administrator Tom Paine had recruited von Braun for the DC job. Paine wanted to garner support for a large-scale mission to Mars and a new space shuttle program. Von Braun would spearhead the effort, promoting the large and expensive projects to the political establishment and the general public, convincing them that they were worthwhile investments. With public support for NASA programs declining after the Apollo missions, it was a tall order. And Paine hoped von Braun could stir up the same type of enthusiasm that he had generated for the moon-landing program.

But von Braun himself was not convinced. He knew better than anyone the costs of a large-scale mission to Mars and a big shuttle program. He thought it was more feasible to focus on a space station and a smaller shuttle program. Unlike the expendable Saturn V rocket and its Apollo capsules, a reusable shuttle could drastically reduce the cost of spaceflight. Within the agency, von Braun lobbied for a more conservative approach that kept costs down in order to make a small shuttle program sustainable. His view was unpopular at NASA, where enthusiasm for a big shuttle program was high. Even as Congress continued to slash NASA's budget, von Braun's arguments for a smaller, more sustainable shuttle program were mostly ignored.

For some of his new colleagues at NASA headquarters, von Braun's status as a former Nazi was a problem. Others resented his celebrity status. These bitter feelings increasingly impacted his work. Although he was fourth in command at NASA, he was regularly left out of decisions and not invited to meetings. "I've found out up here I'm just another guy with a funny accent," he told a former Huntsville colleague.

Back at the Marshall Space Flight Center, von Braun had been king of his own castle and he'd liked it that way, relishing the role of hero. Now all that was changing.

It had only been three years since the Apollo moon landing, but NASA was entering a new orbit, just out of von Braun's reach. He was unhappy but attempted to hide his growing disappointment. Von Braun's glory days, it seemed, had come to an abrupt end.

Von Braun next to the Saturn V's F-1 engines.

In 1972, desperately wanting to put his experience and talents to work in a meaningful way again, von Braun retired from NASA.

He accepted a job in the private sector, working for the aerospace company Fairchild Industries.

As vice president of engineering and development, he jetted around the world, meeting with Fairchild clients from Western Europe to South America. His new role was unburdened by the responsibility of overseeing a large engineering project like the Saturn V or the tedium of playing politics in Washington. Von Braun was back in the center of the aerospace industry, working for a company developing next-generation communications satellites. Fairchild clients eagerly awaited their chance to meet with the famed engineer to discuss how they could partner with Fairchild and, hopefully, hear stories of his NASA days.

In June 1973, von Braun took time out of his busy work schedule to visit Houston to see his doctor and longtime friend, Jim Maxfield. A physical was required to renew his pilot's license, and his new employer had requested a medical exam, strictly as a formality. Von Braun told Maxfield that he was feeling fine, with the exception of some mild discomfort in his back. An X-ray revealed a suspicious shadow on one of his kidneys. The larger-than-life rocketeer seemed unconcerned, but the fact that his mother had died of colon cancer in 1959 was an undeniable risk factor. Maxfield told von Braun to get examined by a kidney specialist. But von Braun dismissed the warning and went back to work, delaying the follow-up appointment until the end of July. When he finally met with the specialist at Johns Hopkins University Hospital in Baltimore, he was immediately scheduled for surgery. On August 22, von Braun underwent an operation to remove his left kidney and a large malignant tumor. He had cancer, but it did not slow him down. Less than two weeks after surgery, he was back at home and recovering well. He resumed his life and work with all the activities of a healthy man. He was gifted at compartmentalizing things that would overwhelm most people: large rocket projects, emotional strain, and a cancer diagnosis. With a hectic work schedule, adventurous family vacations, and a calendar filled with speaking engagements, von Braun continued to resist his doctor's orders and plowed toward the future with single-minded purpose, just as he always had. When he arrived for a follow-up appointment in August 1975, he expected the examination would take less than an hour.

Von Braun's doctor admitted him to Johns Hopkins Hospital the same day. Two days after that, he underwent surgery for a second time to remove a sizable section of his colon with an advanced tumor.

Von Braun's health steadily declined after his hospitalization as his cancer advanced. Five months later, he was walking with a cane. A year after, he collapsed and would spend some of his remaining time at home, before ultimately being confined to the hospital. Von Braun had to be sedated during the last months of his life to ease his pain. He died at three a.m. on Thursday, June 16, 1977, and was laid to rest the next day in a small private service kept secret from the media and public.

The space race had ended, and both of its iconic champions

had been unable to outrun the same disease: cancer. Korolev, whose identity was a state secret until his death, was celebrated in a lavish state funeral, attended by thousands. Von Braun, on the other hand, who had been a recognizable public figure for most of his life, was buried quietly and without fanfare. Like phases of the moon, the two men had cycled in and out of the darkness during their extraordinary and turbulent lifetimes, without their secrets coming to light until after they were gone.

CHAPTER 42

OUT OF THE SHADOWS

1980

CAMBRIDGE, MASSACHUSETTS

When Harvard Law School student Eli Rosenbaum stepped into a bookstore near the university's campus, he didn't expect to find what would become the focus of his life's work. It was his final year of law school. He had recently concluded an internship at the US Department of Justice, where he worked in the newly formed Office of Special Investigations (OSI). The OSI's mission was finding and deporting former war criminals residing in the United States.

As Rosenbaum browsed the shelves, his eyes landed on a book written by a World War II French Resistance fighter, Jean Michel. His book, *Dora: The Nazi Concentration Camp Where Space Technology Was Born and 30,000 Prisoners Died*, was a memoir of his imprisonment at Camp Dora, published the previous year. It was the first widely available account of the lesser-known Dora concentration camp. Despite the horrors there, the tragedies at other camps like Auschwitz had dominated headlines about the Holocaust. American soldiers who had served in Germany heard about Camp Dora or served in its liberation, but their stories never became front-page headlines. The story of the camp and its adjacent Mittelwerk factory slipped into the pages of history unnoticed. It seems incomprehensible, but until Michel's book was published, the gruesome details about the brutality inside Mittelwerk had never been publicly available.

Rosenbaum later returned to the same bookstore and purchased another recently published title, *The Rocket Team*, by Frederick I. Ordway III and Mitchell Sharpe. The book chronicled von Braun's V-2 group from their earliest days at the Peenemünde rocket facility through their more recent work for NASA. Ordway and Sharpe interviewed von Braun's inner circle, and the candor of those conversations astonished Rosenbaum. The comments of one man named Arthur Rudolph caught his attention. He was a longtime member of von Braun's team and one of the Paperclip engineers. Previously, Rudolph had served as operations director of Mittelwerk. His statements to investigators in the war crimes trial of Georg Rickhey, former general manager of Mittelwerk, helped get Rickhey acquitted.

In Ordway and Sharpe's book, Rudolph recounted an incident from 1943. He was called away from a New Year's Eve party to oversee a group of men who were moving a load of heavy rocket equipment. Rudolph noted feeling some frustration at having to leave the celebration and venture out into the frigid night. Because Rosenbaum had read Michel's book, *Dora*, he realized something that set his teeth on edge. "The men that he used to move the rocket parts, they would have been slaves," Rosenbaum later said, "and they were not enjoying some nice party. I just thought that was really, really callous."

After graduation from law school, Rosenbaum accepted a job at OSI and shared his concerns with Deputy Director Neal Sher, who warned his new colleague about the difficulties in pursuing someone like Rudolph. Von Braun and company were heroes to millions of people in America and around the world. The fact that the US had hired Hitler's best engineers to help build missiles had been disclosed while the von Braun team was still at Fort Bliss in the late 1940s. It was decades-old news, glossed over by the incredible achievements of the Apollo moon missions.

But Rosenbaum couldn't forget what he had read in those two books. Something wasn't right. And despite the fact that investigating such a powerful and well-respected person could prove pointless, no one was above the law. The Office of Special Investigations approved Rosenbaum's request to launch an inquiry into Arthur Rudolph.

At that time, Rudolph was in his mid-seventies, living with his wife, Martha, in San Jose, California. He had legally entered the United States in 1949 using the same method as von Braun and the others in Fort Bliss—by first entering Mexico to receive a visa, and then crossing back into the United States. Rudolph had become a naturalized citizen in 1954. Since his top secret arrival in the United States under Operation Paperclip, the mechanical engineer had enjoyed a storied career that reached its zenith when he was named Saturn V project director. After his retirement from the agency in 1969, NASA awarded Rudolph the Distinguished Service Medal, the agency's highest honor.

During multiple interrogations in 1982 and 1983, Rosenbaum and Neal Sher questioned Rudolph. He admitted that he had requested prison labor to increase production efficiency at Mittelwerk. Additional evidence, which included classified army documents and the Nordhausen trial transcripts from 1947, revealed Rudolph's direct involvement in the profound human suffering at Mittelwerk. Rosenbaum, Sher, and the OSI concluded that Rudolph had "mercilessly utilized the slave labor pool to meet production quotas . . . and that he had the rank and authority which he used to participate in the persecution of the prisoners."

He had also witnessed a mass murder. Rudolph was present at the hanging of a group of Dora inmates who were suspected of sabotage. According to one report, Rudolph ordered the other prisoners to watch. OSI argued that the unspeakable act of forcing prisoners to observe the murder of their fellow inmates was "a form of terror." Understandably, Rudolph had withheld these grisly details when he was first selected for Operation Paperclip.

The evidence gathered by Rosenbaum and Sher was overwhelming. There was no proof that Rudolph had personally ordered or committed murders, but the OSI concluded that he was not without responsibility, either.

To avoid an American trial, Rudolph accepted a deal. In 1984 he renounced his US citizenship and returned to Germany. A German investigation into whether Rudolph should stand trial for war crimes ultimately concluded that there was not enough evidence. In Germany, the statute of limitations for a number of Nazi crimes had expired. However, under the terms of Rudolph's deal with OSI, he was allowed to retain his US government retirement income, in addition to health care and social security benefits. Rudolph's NASA commendation for distinguished service still stands.

In mid-October 1984, American newspaper readers were stunned to learn of Rudolph's involvement in concentration camp atrocities, especially because he had risen to an esteemed position at NASA. The Mittelwerk story had never been widely publicized in the US, so most people were learning about it for the first time. Of course, Rudolph had not been the only Paperclip alumnus with ties to Mittelwerk. His exposure had inadvertently rekindled questions about Wernher von Braun. The Apollo program mastermind had been dead nearly eight years, but the secret of his personal connection to Mittelwerk was about to be uncovered.

In 1985, journalist Linda Hunt began investigating Operation Paperclip, as well as the records of the scientists, engineers, and technicians who had been involved. She filed Freedom of Information Act (FOIA) requests with the US government that led to the release of previously classified documents. Von Braun's rank as a decorated major in Hitler's SS was finally exposed, as was the fact that the US government knew about his SS membership but had classified it.

As time passed, historians and academics dug deeper into the story, painstakingly evaluating historical records and combing through archives in the US and Germany. Documents signed by von Braun at Mittelwerk showed that he had known about forced labor in the secret V-2 factory. He calculated the most efficient ratio between skilled workers and concentration camp prisoners. Although he was ordered to make such calculations as part of his job, he was still complicit in the atrocities. He had known about the use of forced labor but had chosen, out of fear or self-preservation, like so many bystanders during World War II, to keep silent.

CHAPTER 43

ALL THAT REMAINS

It's worth considering what might have happened if von Braun had still been alive when Eli Rosenbaum investigated Arthur Rudolph. Would he have been implicated and deported as well? Von Braun had always been a somewhat controversial figure because of his well-known status as the V-2 architect. But his massive and enduring public appeal, high-level political connections, and undeniable contributions to rocket engineering would have been challenging obstacles for OSI investigators to overcome.

As evidence, consider that in the twenty-first century, despite all that has been disclosed about his past, von Braun remains an icon in spaceflight history as the mastermind of the Apollo moon landing, whose Saturn V rocket never failed. His name continues to grace buildings and awards. Following his death, the International Astronomical Union considered renaming a moon crater after von Braun, but the decision was delayed because of his Nazi background. It wasn't until 1994 that the proposal was finally accepted and the lunar crater formerly known as "Lavoisier D" became known as "Von Braun." A conference room at the headquarters of Elon Musk's aerospace manufacturing company, SpaceX, is also named "Von Braun."

Korolev has been similarly memorialized. Two astronomical craters bear his name, one on the moon and another on the surface of Mars. In Russia, a city is called "Korolev." Yet the famous Russian rocket engineer's groundbreaking contributions to spaceflight remain largely omitted from popular narratives of the space race outside of the spaceflight history community. His quest for the moon, while less controversial than von Braun's, is more obscured.

He was responsible for igniting the space race with the launch of Sputnik and dominated the competition during its early years, but few people apart from aerospace professionals, historians, and space-race buffs know his name. This seems ironic, given that Korolev also invented a world-changing weapon, the ICBM—technology that jeopardizes millions of innocent lives on Earth with its capacity to carry nuclear warheads over thousands of miles.

Sergei Korolev, mastermind of the Soviet space program.

Korolev's other lasting achievements, the Soyuz rocket and space capsule, are still in use today. The Soyuz program may have begun with the tragic death of Cosmonaut Komarov, but the system was later perfected by the Russians, becoming an indispensable tool in modern spaceflight, especially for Americans. In 2011, the US ended its space shuttle program when Space Shuttle Atlantis landed for the last time. Thereafter, the only way for American astronauts to reach the International Space Station (ISS) was by paying for a ride aboard Russia's Soyuz. It would be nine years before the US began to reclaim independence from the Soyuz by replacing its space shuttle with a new vehicle. A historic partnership between NASA and the private aerospace company SpaceX resulted in the development of the Falcon 9 rocket and its Crew Dragon space capsule. In May 2020, aboard this newly designed spacecraft, American astronauts once again successfully launched to the ISS from Cape Canaveral. If all goes according to plan, NASA's latest space transportation vehicle, the Space Launch System (SLS), will carry American astronauts back to the moon, and possibly on to Mars by the 2030s.

These next-generation space vehicles are designed to be reusable, drastically lowering equipment costs, removing a major barrier to future space exploration.

How remarkable to consider that all this incredible technology was first imagined by two engineers who dared to dream of voyages to the moon and Mars as early as the 1930s. Equally remarkable is the vast number of secrets, lies, and hidden scandals at the heart of their quests. Yet rarely, if ever, are these stories discussed in classroom history books, because so much of the story was buried for years to protect governments from being held accountable for their actions. Identities were concealed. The contributions of women and people of color who dared to defy race and gender stereotypes went unacknowledged. Files were classified and secret operations undertaken. Documents were buried by the ton in a secret mountain cave. And thousands of concentration camp prisoners, whose lives were forfeited in the advancement of rocket technology, were forgotten.

For these reasons, the hidden history of the space race is a cautionary tale for the next generation of rocketeers and explorers. Scientific advancement comes at a price, and civilizations must weigh every choice against a full knowledge of the past—its accomplishments and its atrocities.

AUTHOR'S NOTE

After two years of reading formerly classified documents and interviewing experts, historians, and archivists from around the world, I had one question that remained unanswered: Was Wernher von Braun a genius worthy of praise for his role in the space race, or was he a privileged man who never suffered any consequences for the lives lost in pursuit of his dream? In search of answers, I traveled to some of the places where the deep history of the space race was buried.

I began in Huntsville, home of the Marshall Space Flight Center and the US Space & Rocket Center (USSRC), where von Braun's influence is everywhere. The Saturn V Hall within the USSRC museum houses the massive rocket, which is suspended overhead. I walked beneath von Braun's masterpiece, astounded by its size and humbled by what America had achieved in the space race. I was so overwhelmed by the scale of the Saturn V, I hardly noticed its great-grandfather, the black-and-white V-2 missile, standing in a nearby corner. It was a surreal experience to see both rockets—one a humanitarian tool of science, the other a weapon of war—within the same exhibit, knowing that one would never have existed without the other.

At the Deutsches Museum in Munich, I spent two days in its vast archives, poring over photographs and leafing through the personal diaries of men who worked with von Braun, like Walter Dornberger. Some of the photographs I found in their extensive collection are included in this book.

My next stop was Nordhausen, where I toured the Mittelwerk tunnels and visited the Camp Dora memorial and museum. I was one of only a handful of tourists exploring the sprawling property and often found myself alone in a silent and disturbingly beautiful place. Spring had come to central Germany, and there were flowers everywhere.

Inside the museum, Nazi cruelty at the Mittelwerk V-2 factory and Camp Dora was on display in artifacts and multimedia exhibits. In filmed testimonials, former camp prisoners told stories of the trauma they endured and somehow managed to survive. A glass display case contained a small piece of wood, about the size of a Magic Marker, with a wire attached. The device was placed between the teeth of prisoners who were about to be hanged and secured behind their head with the wire so they could not cry out.

I left the museum and made my way to the Mittelwerk tunnel entrance, opposite the museum.

Inside it was pitch-black until our guide threw a switch, and dim floodlights lit the huge chamber, which still smelled of dust and metal. Our small group walked carefully along a narrow steel footbridge with a railing, suspended over piles of debris. As we wound through the old underground factory, skeletons of exploded rocket parts littered either side of the footbridge, and our guide repeatedly warned us to watch our step. Decades later, the tunnels are still dangerous—and cold. It was early April and I was freezing in spite of the wool sweater, jacket, and hat I was wearing. The prisoners forced to work inside there were never fortunate enough to have warm clothes like mine. I was relieved when the tour ended and we finally exited the tunnel.

My last stop that day was the hillside crematorium, a small brick building with a large chimney. The smoke from its furnaces would have been visible from much of the camp. Beside it, a landscaped memorial marks a mass grave where the ashes of thousands of people were shoveled into piles and forgotten. I could not bring myself to enter the building.

After my time in Nordhausen, I traveled north to the Baltic Coast to visit the Peenemünde Historical Technical Museum, housed in what remains of the rocket facility built for von Braun by the German army. The museum invites visitors to consider the connections between morality and technological advancement. At the end of my tour, I saw a small bust of von Braun near another exhibit dedicated to the legendary engineer. A pair of clear cylinders, approximately three feet tall, stood side by side. One was labeled *Ruthless*, the other, *Ingenious*. The display card read:

> *Wernher von Braun was portrayed as enthusiast,*
> *dreamer, careerist, militarist, and nationalist. How do you*

estimate his personality—ruthless technician [stopping] at nothing[15], or as an ingenious realizer of spaceflight?

It was an invitation for visitors to grapple with the complexity of von Braun's undeniable contributions to spaceflight. The "ballots" were round cardboard disks that looked like drink coasters. I took one and considered my answer. What makes someone a villain? Can good works and world-changing achievements that advance science absolve a person from complicity in horrific crimes? What are the consequences of ignoring history, of burying it, of not retelling it for the next generation? Perhaps there is more than one answer. Standing there, I realized that after two years of searching for some understanding of Wernher von Braun, I had found mine.

I wonder: Which cylinder would you choose?

---

15 The card's English translation reads, "sticking at nothing."

ACKNOWLEDGMENTS

Books, like rockets, are built in stages by teams. I found support at every stage of this book's development from these fine people:

To my intrepid agent, Ammi-Joan Paquette at Erin Murphy Literary Agency, and my patient editor at Balzer & Bray, Kristin Daly Rens—thank you for helping me tell this story. Thanks also to editorial assistant Caitlin Johnson, for help with photo permissions and so much more. I was also fortunate to benefit from the expertise of skilled copyeditors Renee Cafiero and Valerie Shea.

Heartfelt thanks to Michael Neufeld, historian emeritus at the Smithsonian National Air and Space Museum, and Asif Siddiqi, history professor at Fordham University, for their vast body of academic work that reveals the lives and times of Wernher von Braun and Sergei Korolev. Both these world-class scholars generously shared their insight with me across numerous detailed telephone interviews. Garret McDonald fact-checked the manuscript and offered valuable insight as well. Thank you, Garret.

I am indebted to the following people for their time and perspectives during personal interviews, as they shed light on a complicated and fascinating era in world history: Bill Adams, Homer Hickam,

Jim Jenkins, Monique Laney, Joyce Neighbors, and Bob Schmiedeskamp.

I would also like to thank the communications and archival staff of the US Space & Rocket Center in Huntsville, Alabama, for hosting me at their wonderful museum, arranging interviews with primary sources, and for providing access to their collection of von Braun's papers: Patricia Ammons, Diane M. Brown, Audrey Glasgow, Carolyn Lawson, Allison Overfield, Holly Ralston, and Edward C. Stewart III.

At the Huntsville-Madison County Public Library, Heather Adkins and Shalis Worthy provided archival photo assistance. David Hitt of the Huntsville/Madison County Historical Society answered questions about Huntsville's agrarian history. Thank you.

During my research trip across Germany, Dr. Matthias Röschner, Research Associate and Deputy Head of Archives, was my host at the Deutsches Museum/Archives in Munich. He gathered primary resource material that included photographs and letters of Walter Dornberger and others who worked closely with von Braun. At the Mittelbau-Dora Museum in Nordhausen, Stefanie Taeger, Jörg Kulbe, and Marvin Keitel answered many questions during my tour of the camp and its museum. Danke schoen.

Special thanks go to Jane Adkisson at Pack Memorial Library in Asheville, North Carolina. Her cheerful assistance with countless interlibrary loan requests cleared the path for my early research. Thank you, Jane!

ACKNOWLEDGMENTS

I am also deeply indebted to the Highlights Foundation. Their generous scholarship program made it possible for me to attend a nonfiction writing workshop at their Boyds Mills, Pennsylvania, campus in 2018. With guidance from workshop leaders Deborah Heiligman, Elizabeth Partridge, and Barbara Kerley, I framed the first draft of this book.

My spirits were buoyed daily by the outpouring of practical advice and encouragement from close friends and fellow writers. Thanks also to: Lauren, Cheyenne, and Zoey Azadan, Elaine Barnes, Kim and John Counter, Joseph D'Agnese, Janet Daniels, Alan Gratz, Kristin Jackson, Denise Kiernan, Don Stutts, Ashleigh Tucker, and Paula Yoo.

To my quirky and fiercely independent bookselling colleagues at Malaprop's Bookstore & Café in Asheville, North Carolina, who patiently endured hours of enthusiastic ramblings about the space race (while they tried to work), thanks, y'all.

My aunt, Mary Keener Tatham, lent her expertise and insight as a former educator to the manuscript. Thank you, auntie.

Casey McCormick's boundless optimism, enduring support, and love make anything seem possible. Thanks, Case.

Finally, to my fearless and talented mom, Marty Keener Cherrix, who read every word of every draft and whose unwavering reassurances ("Bird by bird, Aim") kept me going through the toughest of days; how can "thank you" ever be enough? I love you to the moon and back.

BIBLIOGRAPHY

Books

(Pagination in electronic books does not match the print book. Therefore, I cite chapters rather than pages for ebook sources).

Applebaum, Anne. *Gulag: A History.* New York: Anchor Books, 2004.

Barbour, John. *Footprints on the Moon.* New York: Associated Press, 1969.

Bode, Volkhard, and Gerhard Kaiser. *Building Hitler's Missiles: Traces of History at Peenemünde.* Translated by Katy Derbyshire. Berlin: Christoph Links Verlag, 2008.

Brzezinski, Matthew. *Red Moon Rising: Sputnik and the Hidden Rivalries That Ignited the Space Age.* New York: Times Books, 2007.

Cadbury, Deborah. *Space Race: The Battle to Rule the Heavens.* New York: Harper Perennial, 2007.

Chertok, Boris. *Rockets and People.* Vol. 1, edited by Asif A. Siddiqi. The NASA History Series. Washington, DC: NASA History Office, 2005.

———. *Rockets and People: Creating a Rocket Industry.* Vol. 2, edited by Asif A. Siddiqi. The NASA History Series. Washington, DC: NASA History Office, 2006.

———. *Rockets and People: Hot Days of the Cold War.* Vol. 3, edited by Asif A. Siddiqi. The NASA History Series. Washington, DC: NASA History Office, 2005.

Cooper, L. Gordon, and Bruce B. Henderson. *Leap of Faith: An Astronaut's Journey into the Unknown.* New York: Open Road Integrated Media, 2000.

BIBLIOGRAPHY

Doran, Jamie, and Piers Bizony. *Starman: The Truth Behind the Legend of Yuri Gagarin*. New York: Walker & Company, 2011. Ebook.

Dornberger, Walter. *V-2: The Nazi Rocket Weapon*. New York: Ballantine Books, 1954.

Glenn, John, and Nick Taylor. *John Glenn: A Memoir*. New York: Bantam Books, 1999. Ebook.

Hansen, James R., ed. *Dear Neil Armstrong: Letters to the First Man on the Moon from All Mankind*. West Layfayette, IN: Purdue University Press, 2020.

Hardesty, Von, and Gene Eisman. *Epic Rivalry: The Inside Story of the Soviet and American Space Race*. Foreword by Sergei Khrushchev. Washington, DC: National Geographic, 2007.

Harford, James. *Korolev: How One Man Masterminded the Soviet Drive to Beat America to the Moon*. New York: Wiley, 1999.

Hickham, Homer H., Jr. *Rocket Boys: A Memoir*. New York: Delacorte Press, 1998. Ebook.

Hoegh, Lt.-Col. Leo A. *Timberwolf Tracks: The History of the 104th Infantry Division*, Plano, TX: Arcole Publishing, 2017. Ebook.

Jackson, Libby. *Galaxy Girls: 50 Amazing Stories of Women in Space*. New York: Harper Design, an Imprint of HarperCollinsPublishers, 2017.

Jacobsen, Annie. *Operation Paperclip: The Secret Intelligence Program That Brought Nazi Scientists to America*. New York: Back Bay Books, 2015.

Jenks, Andrew. *The Cosmonaut Who Couldn't Stop Smiling: The Life and Legend of Yuri Gagarin*. DeKalb, IL: Northern Illinois University Press, 2014.

Johnson, Katherine. *Reaching for the Moon: The Autobiography of NASA Mathematician Katherine Johnson*. New York: Atheneum Books for Young Readers, 2019.

Kelly, Scott. *Endurance: A Year in Space, a Lifetime of Discovery*. New York: Alfred A. Knopf, 2017. Ebook.

Khrushchev, Nikita. *Khrushchev Remembers*. Edited and translated by Strobe Talbott. New York: Little, Brown & Company, 1970.

——— and Stephen Shenfield. *Memoirs of Nikita Khruschchev: Reformer, 1945–1964*. Edited by Sergei Khrushchev. Translated by George

Shriver. Vol. 2. University Park, PA: Pennsylvania State University Press, 2006.

Khruschchev, Sergei. *Nikita Khrushchev and the Creation of a Superpower.* Translated by Shirley Benson. University Park, PA: Pennsylvania State University Press, 2003.

Kranz, Gene. *Failure Is Not an Option.* New York: Simon & Schuster, 2000.

Laney, Monique. *German Rocketeers in the Heart of Dixie.* New Haven, CT: Yale University Press, 2015.

Logsdon, John M. *The Penguin Book of Outer Space Exploration: NASA and the Incredible Story of Human Spaceflight.* Foreword by Bill Nye. New York: Penguin Books, 2018.

McGovern, James. *Crossbow and Overcast: The True Story of the V-2 Rocket— The Deadly Secret Weapon That Almost Won the War.* New York: Paperback Library, 1966.

Medaris, Bruce, ed. *Countdown to Decision.* New York: G. P. Putnam's Sons, 1960.

Neufeld, Michael J. *The Rocket and the Reich: Peenemünde and the Coming of the Ballistic Missile Era.* New York: Free Press, 1995.

———. *Spaceflight: A Concise History.* Cambridge, MA: MIT Press, 2018.

———. *Von Braun: Dreamer of Space, Engineer of War.* New York: Vintage Books, 2008.

Ordway, Frederick L., and Mitchell K. Sharpe. *The Rocket Team.* New York: Thomas Y. Crowell Co., 1979.

Rhea, John. *Roads to Space: An Oral History of the Soviet Space Program.* Translated by Peter Berlin. New York: McGraw-Hill Companies, 1995.

Romanov, A. *The Apprenticeship of a Space Pioneer.* Moscow: Mir Publishers, 1975.

———. *Spacecraft Designer: The Story of Sergei Korolev.* Moscow: Novosti Press Agency Publishing House, 1976.

Scott, David, and Alexei Leonov, with Christine Toomey. *Two Sides of the Moon: Our Story of the Cold War Space Race.* Foreword by Neil Armstrong. New York: Thomas Dunne Books, 2013. Ebook.

Shepard, Alan, and Deke Slayton, with Jay Barbree. *Moon Shot.* Open Road Integrated Media, 2011. Ebook.

Siddiqi, Asif A. *The Red Rockets' Glare: Spaceflight and the Soviet Imagination, 1857–1957.* Cambridge, UK: Cambridge University Press, 2013.

———. *The Soviet Space Race with Apollo.* Gainesville: University of Florida Press, 2000.

———. *Sputnik and the Soviet Space Challenge.* Gainesville: University of Florida Press, 2000.

Sparrow, Giles, Judith John, and Chris McNab, eds. *The Illustrated Encyclopedia of Space & Space Exploration: Discovering the Secrets of the Universe.* New York: Metro Books, 2014.

Stone, Robert, and Alan Andres. *Chasing the Moon: The People, the Politics, and the Promise That Launched America into the Space Age.* New York: Ballantine Books, 2019.

Stuhlinger, Ernst, and Frederick I. Ordway III. *Wernher von Braun: Crusader for Space: A Biographical Memoir.* Malabar, FL: Krieger Publishing Company, 1994.

Thompson, Neal. *Light This Candle: The Life and Times of Alan Shepard.* New York: Three Rivers Press, 2004. Ebook.

Ward, Bob. *Dr. Space: The Life of Wernher von Braun.* New York: Naval Institute Press, 2013.

Watkins, Billy. *Apollo Moon Missions: The Unsung Heroes.* Foreword by Frederich Haise. Lincoln: Bison Books/University of Nebraska Press, 2007.

Wolfe, Tom. *The Right Stuff.* New York: Picador, 2008.

Articles

Carmichael, Neil. "A Brief History of the Berlin Crisis of 1961." www .archives.gov.

Clauser, F. H. "Preliminary Design of a World-Circling Spaceship." Santa Monica, CA: Rand Corporation, May 2, 1946. www.rand.org.

Cosgrove, Ben. "After the Fall: Photos of Hitler's Bunker and the Ruins of Berlin." www.time.com/3524807/after-the-fall-photos-of-hitlers-bunker -and-the-ruins-of-berlin.

"Death of Yury Gagarin Demystified 40 Years On." *RT,* June 14, 2013.

www.rt.com/news/gagarin-death-truth-revealed-674.

Dejevsky, Mary. "The First Woman in Space: People Shouldn't Waste Money on Wars." *Guardian*, March 29, 2017. www.theguardian.com/global -development-professionals-network/2017/mar/29/valentina -tereshkova-first-woman-in-space-people-waste-money-on-wars.

Dungan, T. "Antwerp: City of Sudden Death." www.v2rocket.com/start /chapters/antwerp.html.

Dunnavant, Bob. "Mars Landing Decision Near, Says von Braun." *Decatur Daily*, July 25, 1969. www.newspaperarchive.com/decatur-daily-jul-25 -1969-p-1.

Evans, Ben. "'The Saddest Moment': The Story of America's First Space Walk," Part 2. www.americaspace.com/2015/05/31/the-saddest -moment-the-story-of-americas-first-spacewalk-part-2.

Fox, Karen. "NASA's Van Allen Probes Spot an Impenetrable Barrier in Space." www.nasa.gov/content/goddard/van-allen-probes-spot -impenetrable-barrier-in-space.

Garamone, Jim. "Remembering the Holocaust." Armed Forces Press Service. https://archive.defense.gov/news/newsarticle.aspx?id=45049

Gee, Alison. "Pushinka: A Cold War Puppy the Kennedys Loved." *BBC World Service*, January 6, 2014. www.bbc.com/news /magazine-24837199.

Godwin, Richard. "One Giant . . . Lie? Why So Many People Still Think the Moon Landings Were Faked." *Guardian*, July 10, 2019. www.theguardian.com/science/2019/jul/10/one-giant-lie-why-so-many -people-still-think-the-moon-landings-were-faked.

Hollingham, Richard. "The World's Oldest Scientific Satellite Is Still in Orbit." BBC, October 6, 2017. www.bbc.com/future/article /20171005-the-worlds-oldest-scientific-satellite-is-still-in-orbit.

Holton, Sean. "U.S. Space Program Arose from Nazi Germany's Ashes." *Orlando Sentinel*, April 30, 1995. www.chicagotribune.com/news /ct-xpm-1995-04-30-9504300235-story.html.

Lang, Daniel. "A Reporter at Large: White Sands." *The New Yorker*, July 24, 1948.

Latson, Jennifer. "The Sad Story of Laika, the First Dog Launched into

Orbit." *Time,* November 3, 2014. www.time.com/3546215/laika-1957.

Leibson, Art. "118 V-2 Experts Stationed in E.P." *El Paso Times,* December 4, 1946. www.newspapers.com.

Leonov, Alexei. "The Nightmare of Voskhod 2." *Air & Space,* January 2005. www.airspacemag.com/space/the-nightmare-of -voskhod-2-8655378.

McClendon, Sarah. "German Scientists in El Paso Blasted." *El Paso Times,* July 1, 1947. www.newspapers.com.

O'Toole, Thomas, and Mary Thornton. "Road to Departure by Ex-Nazi Engineer." *Washington Post,* November 4, 1984. www.washingtonpost .com/archive/politics/1984/11/04/road-to-departure-of-ex-nazi -engineer/729f5dd6-e009-4265-bbc4-21096e5e526f/.

"Protection Shelter for Storms and War." *Wilkes-Barre Times Leader,* March 5, 1958. www.newspapers.com.

Remme, Tilman. "The Battle for Berlin in World War II." www.bbc.co.uk /history/worldwars/wwtwo/berlin_01.shtml.

Robinson, Donald R. "The Story behind the Explorers." *This Week Magazine,* April 13, 1958, www.newspapersonline.com.

Siddiqi, Asif A. "The First Woman in Earth Orbit." *Spaceflight,* Vol. 51, January 2009, 20–21.

———. "The First Woman in Earth Orbit: Transcripts Give New Perspective on Vostok-6 Mission." https://faculty.fordham.edu/siddiqi /writings/p28a_siddiqi_vostok-6_mission.pdf.

Tedeschi, Diane. "How Much Did von Braun Know, and When Did He Know It?" *Air & Space,* January 1, 2008. www.airspacemag.com/space /a-amp-s-interview-michael-j-neufeld-23236520.

Von Braun, Werhner. "Man Will Conquer Space Soon." *Collier's,* March 22, 1952.

Von Braun, Wernher, as told to Curtis Mitchell. "Space Man: The Story of My Life." *American Weekly,* Vol. 7, Part 1, July 20, 1958; Vol. 10, Part 2, July 27, 1958; Vol. 12, Part 3, August 3, 1958.

Wellerstein, Alex. "Remembering Laika, Space Dog and Soviet Hero." *New Yorker,* November 3, 2017. www.newyorker.com/tech/annals-of -technology/remembering-laika-space-dog-and-soviet-hero.

Zak, Anatoly. "The R-7 Interconinental Ballistic Missile." Russian Space Web. www.russianspaceweb.com/r7.html.

Documentary Films and Videos

Dog That Orbited the Earth, The. BBC Witness History. https://www.bbc.com/news/av/magazine-41901604/the-dog-that -orbited-the-earth.

Equinox, season 2, episode 1, "The Engines That Came in from the Cold." Written and directed by Dan Clifton, aired 2001, on Channel 4 (UK).

He Conquered Space. Directed by Daniel B. Polin, written by Daniel B. Polin and Perry Wolff, Discovery Channel, 1996.

Mission Control: The Unsung Heroes of Apollo. Directed by David Fairhead. March 14, 2017.

NASA's Look at 50 Years of Apollo: "Apollo 8: Around the Moon and Back," episode 3. NASA. www.youtube.com/watch?v=Wfd0oC3eFWw.

The Russian Right Stuff, episode 1, "The Invisible Spaceman." David Dugan, series producer. Aired 1991, NOVA/PBS.

Sputnik Declassified. Written and directed by Rushmore DeNooyer. Aired 2007, NOVA/PBS.

Other Reports, Papers, and Transcripts

Clauser, F. H. "Preliminary Design of a World-Circling Spaceship." Santa Monica, CA: Rand Corporation, May 2, 1946. www.rand.org/pubs /special_memoranda/SM11827.html.

Feigin, Judy. "The Office of Special Investigations: Striving for Accountability in the Aftermath of the Holocaust." Mark M. Richard, ed. The Office of Special Investigations, December 2008, 333. http://storage.lib.uchicago.edu/pres/2015/pres2015-0270.pdf.

Kezirian, Michael T., Joseph Pelton, and Tommaso Sgobba. "The Russian R-16 Nedelin Disaster: An Historical Analysis of Failed Safety Management." Journal of Space Safety Engineering, Volume 2, No. 2. December 2015. www.iaass.space-safety.org/wp-content/uploads /sites/24/2015/07/JSSE-VOL.-2-NO.-2-DECEMBER-2015-LR-THE

-RUSSIAN-R-16-NEDELIN-DISASTER.pdf.

"Technical Air-to-Ground Voice Transmission (GOSS NET 1) from the Apollo 11 mission." www.hq.nasa.gov/alsj/a11/a11transcript_tec.html.

Woods, W. David, Johannes Kemppanen, Alexander Turhanov, and Lennox J. Waugh. *Apollo Flight Journal*, Apollo 13, Day 3, Part 2: "Houston, We've Had a Problem." www.history.nasa.gov/afj/ap13fj/08day3 -problem.html.

Woods, W. David, Robin Wheeler, and Ian Roberts. *Apollo Corrected Transcript*, Apollo 10, Day 5, Part 19: "We Is Down Among Them." https://history.nasa.gov/afj/ap10fj/as10-day5-pt19.html.

Websites and Blogs

The Berlin Wall: A Multimedia History. "August 13, 1961, Through the Eyes of a Border Guard: Peter Guba." www.the-berlin-wall.com.videos /berlin-contemporary-witnesses-eyes-of-a-border-guard-808.

"The Count of Pearl Harbor Deaths." Pearlharbor.org. https://visitpearlharbor.org/how-many-pearl-harbor-deaths-were-there.

"Documenting Numbers of Victims of the Holocaust and Nazi Persecution." https://encyclopedia.ushmm.org/content/en/article/documenting -numbers-of-victims-of-the-holocaust-and-nazi-persecution.

Eisenhower Library online archives. www.eisenhowerlibrary.gov/research /online-documents.

"Gas Chambers." www.auschwitz.org/en/history/auschwitz-and-shoah/gas -chambers.

"Gemini: Bridge to the Moon." NASA.gov. www.nasa.gov/specials/gemini _gallery.

"Heinrich Himmler." https://encyclopedia.ushmm.org/content/en/article /heinrich-himmler.

Jenks, Andrew. "The Russian Icarus: How Gagarin Became Cosmonaut #1." Russian History Blog, February 25, 2011. www.russianhistoryblog .org/2011/02/the-russian-icarus-how-gagarin-became-cosmonaut-1.

"Mittelbau-Dora." www.holocaust.org.uk/mittelbau-dora.

"Mittelbau Dora Concentration Camp." www.johngalione.com /timberwolf415b003.htm.

"Mittelbau-Dora in the National Socialist Concentration Camp System."
    Mittelbau-Dora Memorial. www.buchenwald.de/en/29.

"Mittelbau Main Camp: In Depth." https://encyclopedia.ushmm.org
    /content/en/article/mittelbau-main-camp-in-depth.

"Redstone and Atlas." NASA History. www.history.nasa.gov/SP-4201
    /ch1-5.htm.

"Research Starters: Worldwide Deaths in World War II."
    www.nationalww2museum.org/students-teachers/student-resources
    /research-starters/research-starters-worldwide-deaths-world-war.

"Sergei Korolev: Father of the Soviet Union's Success in Space." www.esa
    .int/About_Us/ESA_history/50_years_of_humans_in_space/Sergei
    _Korolev_Father_of_the_Soviet_Union_s_success_in_space.

"V-2 Missile." Smithsonian National Air and Space Museum. https://
    airandspace.si.edu/collection-objects/missile-surface-surface-v-2-4.

"Work in the Gulag." www.gulaghistory.org/nps/onlineexhibit/stalin
    /work.php.

ENDNOTES

Chapter 1: The Osenberg List

Page 3: The Polish lab technician's discovery described: Jacobsen, *Operation Paperclip: The Secret Intelligence Program That Brought Nazi Scientists to America*, 41.

Page 4: Dr. Werner Osenberg described: ibid.

Page 5: five times the speed of sound: Jacobsen, 7.

Page 6: This fundamental . . . capitalism: Garret McDonald, correspondence with the author, March 15, 2020.

Page 7: "carry out all . . . restraint": United States Holocaust Memorial Museum website, "The SS," https://encyclopedia.ushmm.org/content/en/article/ss.

Chapter 2: The Honored Nazi

Page 8: Description of china place settings: Jacobsen, 7.

Page 8: The formal affair at the castle: See Jacobsen's note, 464.

Page 9: Knight's Cross of War Service Cross: Neufeld, *Von Braun: Dreamer of Space, Engineer of War*, 187.

Page 10: "The room . . . exhaust": Walter Dornberger quoted in Ordway and Sharpe, *The Rocket Team*, 49.

Page 10: "It was like a streak . . . star": Charles Ostyn's recollections quoted in Dungan, "Antwerp: City of Sudden Death."

Page 11: Some 3,700 civilians were killed: ibid.

Page 11: State of mind of Antwerp's citizens during V-2 bombings: ibid.

Page 11: Von Braun describes his plan to surrender to the Americans:

von Braun as told to Curtis Mitchell, "Space Man: The Story of My Life," Vol. 10, Part 2, *American Weekly*, July 27, 1958.

Page 12: Himmler was the key . . . Europe: United States Holocaust Memorial Museum, https://encyclopedia.ushmm.org/content/en/article /heinrich-himmler.

Page 12: Von Braun's arrest: Neufeld, *Von Braun*, 172.

Chapter 3: Rise of the Rocket Fanatic

Page 14: Von Braun's childhood and lifelong desire to fly to the moon described in Neufeld, *Von Braun*, 21.

Page 15: homemade car: von Braun, "Space Man," *American Weekly*, July 20, 1958, 9.

Page 15: "It swerved this . . . fire": von Braun, ibid., 8.

Page 15: "Whenever I tried . . . life": Emmy von Braun, quoted in Stuhlinger and Ordway, *Wernher von Braun: Crusader for Space*, 11.

Page 16: 124 miles southwest of Berlin: Neufeld, *Von Braun*, 22.

Page 16: "I was . . . equations": von Braun, *He Conquered Space*, documentary film.

Page 16: "What can I do . . . book": von Braun, ibid.

Page 17: "By day I taught . . . lessons": Wernher von Braun quoted in Neufeld, *Von Braun*, 35. See also 483, footnote 33.

Page 19: abandoned munitions dump: Neufeld, *Spaceflight*, 13.

Page 20: "astonishing theoretical knowledge": Dornberger, *V-2: The Nazi Rocket Weapon*, 33.

Page 21: "To me, the army's . . . travel": von Braun quoted in Neufeld, *Von Braun*, 54.

Page 22: local residents . . . land: Bode and Kaiser, *Building Hitler's Missiles*, 22.

Page 22: See Bode and Kaiser for more information about the last days of the Peenemünde village.

Page 22: Von Braun's gift of champagne to a Peenemünde engineer described: Neufeld, *Von Braun*, 94.

Page 23: "My refusal to join . . . activity": von Braun quoted in Cadbury, *Space Race: The Battle to Rule the Heavens*, 53.

Page 23: Nazis murdered . . . conflict: National World War II Museum, "Research Starters: Worldwide Deaths in World War II, www .nationalww2museum.org/students-teachers/student-resources/research -starters/research-starters-worldwide-deaths-world-war.

Page 23: Groups targeted and persecuted by the Nazis described: US Holocaust Memorial Museum, "Documenting Numbers of Victims of the Holocaust and Nazi Persecution," https://encyclopedia.ushmm.org/content/en /article/documenting-numbers-of-victims-of-the-holocaust-and-nazi-persecution.

Chapter 4: Camp Dora

Page 24: felt grateful to have survived the war this far: "Mittelbau Dora Concentration Camp."

Page 24: The corpses of . . . buildings: Hoegh, *Timberwolf Tracks: The History of the 104th Infantry Division, 1942–1945*, 458.

Page 25: "Stacked like cordwood": ibid.

Page 25: "The people were . . . rescued": John Galione in Garamone, "Remembering the Holocaust," Armed Forces Press Service, www .archive.defense.gov/news/newsarticle.aspx?id=45049.

Page 25: sixty thousand people: National Holocaust Centre and Museum, "Mittelbau-Dora."

Page 26: Neufeld describes Kammler's role in building gas chambers at Auschwitz-Birkenau, Majdanek, and Belzec, in *The Rocket and the Reich*, 201.

Page 26: Detailed Auschwitz-Birkenau gas chamber figures: "Gas Chambers," Memorial Museum Auschwitz-Birkenau, www.auschwitz .org/en/history/auschwitz-and-shoah/gas-chambers.

Page 26: Origins and nationalities of prisoners at Camp Dora, "Mittelbau-Dora in the National Socialist Concentration Camp System."

Page 27: not seeing daylight for months: Neufeld, "Mittelbau Main Camp: In Depth," United States Holocaust Memorial Museum, https://

encyclopedia.ushmm.org/content/en/article/mittelbau-main-camp-in-depth.

Page 27: "They were crawling . . . anymore": Albert Van Dijk, Camp Mittelbau-Dora Museum, recorded interview video exhibit, viewed by author, April 5, 2019.

Page 28: death toll average 160 a day: O'Toole and Thornton, "Road to Departure of Ex-Nazi Engineer," www.washingtonpost.com/archive /politics/1984/11/04/road-to-departure-of-ex-nazi-engineer/729f5dd6 -e009-4265-bbc4-21096e5e526f/?noredirect=on&utm_term=.4c50e46f8ee9.

Page 28: fifteen times, Neufeld quoted in Tedeschi, "How Much Did Wernher von Braun Know, and When Did He Know It?"

Page 29: "In view of . . . 2:1": Von Braun's memo quoted in Neufeld, *Von Braun*, 163.

Page 29: Von Braun's implicit guilt in Mittelwerk attrocities: as discussed with Michael Neufeld, senior curator in the Space History Department, Smithsonian National Air and Space Museum, telephone interview with the author, October 4, 2019.

Page 29: he may indeed have been guilty: ibid.

Page 29: Von Braun's ambivalence to the plight of the Jews described in Neufeld, *Von Braun*, 97.

Page 29: Von Braun did not wear . . . correspondence: Neufeld, *Von Braun*, 122.

Page 29: "There was no way around it": von Braun's response as recalled by engineer Hartmut Küchen and quoted from *Peenemünde: Schatten eines Mythos*, M. J. Blockwitz and A. Walter, 1999, in Neufeld, *Von Braun*, 122.

Chapter 5: Betraying Hitler

Page 31: Statistics on the number of Red Army tanks, personnel, and artillery in Remme, "The Battle for Berlin in World War II," www.bbc.co.uk /history/worldwars/wwtwo/berlin_01.shtml.

Page 31: hundreds of thousands . . . children: Cosgrove, "After the Fall: Photos of Hitler's Bunker and the Ruins of Berlin."

Page 33: "I hopped on . . . story": Magnus von Braun quoted in Holton, "U.S. Space Program Arose from Nazi Germany's Ashes."

Page 33: Climate and landscape details at the time of the surrender of the von Braun team, see Dornberger, *V-2*, 235.

Page 33: "They showed up . . . Camels": Magnus von Braun, quoted in Holton, *Chicago Tribune*.

Page 35: von Braun and approximately 350 members of his team: Neufeld, interview with the author, October 4, 2019.

Page 36: Failure of US intelligence to question von Braun about his association with Mittelwerk: as discussed with Neufeld, telephone interview with the author, October 4, 2019.

Page 37: By late afternoon . . . 1945: Neufeld, *Von Braun*, 213.

Page 37: Six members . . . departed, ibid.

Chapter 6: An Innocent Traitor

Page 42: a copy of *Pravda*: Siddiqi, *The Red Rockets' Glare*, 177.

Page 42: a loaf of French bread: ibid.

Page 42: Location of Natalia Korolev during her father's arrest: Asif Siddiqi, telephone interview with the author, March 1, 2019.

Page 42: dressed in dark suits: Siddiqi, *The Red Rockets' Glare*, 155.

Page 42: Black Ravens: Asif Siddiqi, telephone interview with the author, March 1, 2019.

Page 42: listened to music . . . phonograph: ibid.

Page 42: The doorbell rang: Siddiqi, *The Red Rockets' Glare*, 155.

Page 42: Information on NKVD officer weapons per World War II collector Bill Adams: interview with the author, November 26, 2018.

Page 43: NKVD arrest practices: discussed with Asif Siddiqi, interview with the author, March 1, 2019.

Page 43: "I naively gave him . . . other." Ksenia Korolev quoted in *The Russian Right Stuff*, "The Invisible Spaceman," episode 1.

Page 43: "I had golden hair . . . overnight": ibid.

Page 43: broke both . . . jaws: Siddiqi, *The Red Rockets' Glare*, 177.

Page 43: a fifteen-minute deliberation: ibid.

Page 43: notorious Gulag . . . Siberia: "Work in the Gulag," www .gulaghistory.org/nps/onlineexhibit/stalin/work.php.

Page 44: only 217 miles south . . . Arctic Circle: Siddiqi, *The Red Rockets' Glare*, 188.

Page 44: Korolev's childhood and first experience with flight, Harford, 16–18.

Page 44: At seventeen . . . glider: "Sergei Korolev: Father of the Soviet Union's Success in Space."

Page 44: a roofer's apprentice: Romanov, *Spacecraft Designer: The Story of Sergei Korolev*, 12.

Page 45: "Going up in . . . engine": Romanov, 17.

Page 46: the official center . . . missiles: "Sergei Korolev: Father of the Soviet Union's Success in Space."

Page 46: July 1939 . . . prisoners: Siddiqi, *The Red Rockets' Glare*, 188.

Page 46: leaving . . . his head: ibid., 188.

Page 46: spoiled cabbage . . . fish: soup recipe ingredients as remembered by former Gulag prisoner Galina Levinson, quoted in Applebaum, *Gulag: A History*, 206.

Page 46: Korolev developed . . . teeth: Siddiqi, *The Red Rockets' Glare*, 188.

Page 46: Parasite infestations in the Gulag camps: see Applebaum, 202–4.

Page 46: Gulag prisoner clothing: ibid., 176–78, 221–26, 287.

Page 47: Fate of prisoners at Camp Kolyma: Siddiqi, *The Red Rockets' Glare*, 188.

Page 47: He endured . . . fifteen months.: Korolev's letter quoted in Siddiqi, *The Red Rockets' Glare*, 188.

Page 47: "I am convicted . . . organization": Korolev's letter quoted in Cadbury, 85.

Page 47: "I am so very tired . . . situation": ibid., 80.

Page 47: specialized prison laboratory or workshop: *sharashki* as described by Garret McDonald, email correspondence with the author, March 15, 2020.

Page 48: Korolev's year in Kazan after being released from prison: James Harford, *Korolev: How One Man Masterminded the Soviet Drive to Beat America to the Moon*, 63.

Page 51: "the absence of medals . . . fight." Chertok, *Rockets and People*, Vol. 1, 328.

Page 51: "he sank into a deep . . . legs": ibid., 328.

Page 52: Korolev thanked . . . departed: ibid., 329.

Page 52: drove away: ibid., 329.

Page 52: "He wasn't yet . . . himself": ibid., 330.

Chapter 7: Confiscating the Spoils of War

Page 54: 150 former Dora prisoners: James McGovern, *Crossbow and Overcast*, 150.

Page 54: 350 railcars . . . May 31: McGovern, 152.

Page 56: they needed to . . . families: Siddiqi, *The Red Rockets' Glare*, 227.

Page 57: could be useful . . . Union: Ivan Serov's speech recalled in Chertok, *Rockets and People*, Vol. 1, 365.

Page 57: "would be taken . . . wishes"; Chertok, ibid.

Page 57: "We will allow . . . wish"; "No action required . . . trauma"; "it was difficult to . . . seized.": ibid.

Page 58: reportedly remarked . . . self-respect: Siddiqi, *Sputnik and the Soviet Space Challenge*, 42, footnote 74.

Page 58: Description of Soviet banquet hall: Kurt Magnus quoted in Harford, 76.

Page 58: "Fruit was in . . . abundance": ibid.

Page 58: "vodka, vodka, vodka": ibid.

Page 58: "Around one a.m. . . . ended.": Chertok, *Rockets and People*, Vol. 1, 366.

Page 58: "The Russians are . . . away": Irmgard Gröttrup, quoted in Harford, 76, 348 (note 36).

Page 58: Irmgard believed it was a prank: ibid.

Page 58: arriving . . . hundreds.: Chertok, *Rockets and People*, Vol. 1, 366.

Page 58: "The dazed, half-asleep . . . was an order": ibid.

Page 59: Approximately five thousand rocket specialists: Harford, 75. Note that there is some debate about the total number of German scientists deported by the Soviets. Siddiqi suggests the number could have been as high as six thousand. See *Sputnik and Soviet Space Challenge*, 43.

Page 59: abducted and transported . . . Moscow: Harford, 75.

Chapter 8: Back to the USSR

Page 60: "we were horrified": Chertok, *Rockets and People*, Vol. 2, 29.

Page 60: something out of the Stone Age: ibid.

Page 60: "There was dirt . . . ransacked": ibid.

Page 60: overcrowded barracks: Siddiqi, *Sputnik and the Soviet Space Challenge*, 44.

Page 60: 1,700 cities . . . dead: Statistics as reported in Siddiqi, *Sputnik and the Soviet Space Challenge*, 23.

Page 61: lasted nearly a decade: Harford, 94, 151.

Page 61: leaky roofs. The engineers didn't . . . desks: Siddiqi, *Sputnik and the Soviet Space Challenge*, 44.

Page 61: "did not offer his hand": Korolev in a letter to his wife, quoted in Siddiqi, *Sputnik and the Soviet Space Challenge*, 60.

Page 62: silently at first . . . questions: ibid.

Page 62: Kapustin Yar test range described: ibid., 54.

Chapter 9: Space Cowboys

Page 64: POPs (prisoners of peace): Ward, *Dr. Space*, 63.

Page 65: fire hoses, sandbags . . . pillows: ibid., 64.

Page 65: "Frankly, we were . . . so": Wernher von Braun quoted in McGovern, 200.

Page 65: "We were distrusted . . . land"; "Nobody seemed to . . . ridiculous"; "We had been coddled . . . pennies": Wernher von Braun quoted in Ward, 67.

Page 67: Operation Paperclip . . . program: Nature of Operation Paperclip as discussed with Neufeld, October 4, 2019.

Page 67: War Department's decision to keep von Braun's membership in the SS classified: discussed with Neufeld, October 4, 2019.

Page 68: "the brains behind . . . enemies": Art Leibson, "118 V-2 Experts Stationed in E.P."

Page 68: Public disclosure of Operation Paperclip, as discussed with Neufeld, October 4, 2019.

Page 68: "I have never thought . . . synonymous": John Dingell in Sarah

ENDNOTES

McClendon, "German Scientists in El Paso Blasted," *El Paso Times*, July 1, 1947.

Page 69: Visitors drove . . . future: Daniel Lang, "A Reporter at Large: White Sands."

Page 69: nearly seventy V-2 rockets: Hardesty and Eisman, *Epic Rivalry: The Inside Story of the Soviet and American Space Race*, 30.

Page 69: "I had secretly hoped . . . down": von Braun, "Space Man," *American Weekly*, August 3, 1958, 9.

Page 69: "subtlety of a bulldozer": ibid.

Page 70: "I'd never thought of marrying anyone else": Maria von Braun's letter to Wernher von Braun, "Space Man," ibid, 14.

Page 70: He was . . . died: As discussed with Michael Neufeld in a telephone interview with the author, December 20, 2019.

Page 70: Summary of Rickhey's trial: ibid.

Page 71: "I am not acquainted with . . . Mittelwerk": Typescript of von Braun's sworn testimony in the trial of Georg Rickhey, October 14, 1947, Dachau Trials of 1947, 2018-0026, Collection: von Braun Dreamer of Space, Engineer of War [Neufeld], Box Number 6, Folder "WvB/MvBJr-Dora Trial 1947.

Page 73: 370 miles from . . . site. Cadbury, 127.

Page 73: "We can dream . . . dice": Wernher von Braun quoted in Ordway and Sharpe, 361.

Chapter 10: The Cold War

Page 76: forced each other to . . . rival: "Brinkmanship," Encyclopedia Britannica, www.britannica.com/topic/brinkmanship.

Page 77: "War will come . . . radiation": Earl Reichert quoted in "Protection Shelter for Storms and War."

Page 77: Dimensions and materials composing Reichert's bomb shelter: ibid.

Page 77: "You buy life . . . alive": ibid.

Page 80: an American officer in civilian clothes; everything had been . . . officers; eighteen dollars in cash; He answered . . . Mexico: Neufeld, *Von Braun*, 245.

299

Page 81: "was the most valuable . . . spent." Wernher von Braun quoted in Ward, 74.

Chapter 11: Welcome to the Watercress Capital of the World!

Page 82: "a bunch of . . . men": Robert Searcy quoted in Ward, 76.

Page 83: first large-scale . . . fuel: "V-2 Missile."

Page 84: "Free to move around . . . America": Ernst Stuhlinger quoted in Laney, 94.

Page 84: which automatically . . . 1950s: ibid., 127.

Page 84: without assets or a credit history: Ordway and Sharpe, 364.

Page 86: four million subscribers: Hardesty and Eisman, 39.

Page 86: four miles per second . . . sound: von Braun, *Collier's*, March 22, 1952, 25.

Page 86: "From this platform . . . step"; "The job would . . . bomb"; "if we can . . . mankind": ibid., 24.

Page 87: "The US must . . . Union." ibid., 23.

Chapter 12: The Intercontinental Ballistic Missile (ICBM)

Page 88: "Stalin dies after . . . says." *New York Times*, late city edition, front page, March 6, 1953.

Page 88: Korolev grieved Stalin's death: Harford, 234.

Page 89: Abramov describes Korolev's eating habits in Siddiqi, *Sputnik and the Soviet Space Challenge*, 118.

Page 89: R-7 dimensions: Zak, "The R-7 Interconinental Ballistic Missile."

Page 89: three-to-five megaton . . . device: ibid.

Page 91: travel at a . . . world: Siddiqi, *The Red Rockets' Glare*, 241.

Page 93: Exchange of Christmas cards between Korolev and Glushko, Siddiqi, interview with the author, March 1, 2019.

Page 93: constant bickering: Chertok, *Rockets and People*, Vol. 2, 302.

Page 93: "general atmosphere . . . prevailed": ibid.

ENDNOTES

Chapter 13: A Rocket Man in Tomorrowland

Page 94: Von Braun's relationship with Walt Disney: Neufeld, *Von Braun*, 285–90.

Page 94: thirty-eight . . . experts: Ward, 86.

Page 97: "one of the . . . of my life": von Braun quoted in Ward, 86.

Page 98: "Since the advent . . . world": Eisenhower's remarks at the Department of State 1954 Honor Awards Ceremony, October 19, 1954, Eisenhower Library, www.eisenhowerlibrary.gov/eisenhowers/quotes.

Page 98: Eisenhower's fears of a future surprise Soviet attack similar to Pearl Harbor in December 1941: Hardesty and Eisman, 44–45.

Page 98: Pearl Harbor attack statistics: "The Count of Pearl Harbor Deaths," Pearlharbor.org.

Page 99: Eisenhower and Technological Capabilities Panel (TCP): ibid., 44–47.

Page 99: "one of the . . . 20th century." Hardesty and Eisman, 56.

Page 99: "comparable to the . . . bomb": Clauser, "Preliminary Design of a World-Circling Spaceship," 2.

Page 100: Eisenhower and Freedom of Space principle: ibid., 47, 57, 59–60.

Page 100: The IGY's . . . project: Hardesty and Eisman, 59–60.

Chapter 14: A Red Moon Rises

Page 105: "stretched upward . . . aquarium;" "windows covered . . . white paint;" "crowding together at the entrance;": Sergei Khrushchev, *Nikita Khrushchev and the Creation of a Superpower*, 106.

Page 105: "We did everything . . . tasted": Nikita Khruschev from *Khrushchev Remembers*, quoted in Siddiqi, *Challenge to Apollo*, ibid.

Page 106: "Yes, a terrible force . . . Terrible": Nikita Khrushchev quoted in Sergei Khrushchev, *Nikita Khrushchev and the Creation of a Superpower*, 106.

Page 106: "I would like you . . . project": Korolev's conversation with Khrushchev as recalled by his son, Sergei Khrushchev, in ibid., 110.

Page 106: rods protruding on all sides: ibid.

Page 107: "The main . . . country": ibid.

Chapter 15: Army vs. Navy

Page 110: "We had worked hard . . . together": Randy Clinton quoted in *Sputnik Declassified*, NOVA/ PBS special.

Page 110: a superior scientific proposal . . . efficient: Neufeld, interview with the author, October 4, 2019.

Page 111: Engineer Randy Clinton described hiding the satellite in the trunk of his automobile, *Sputnik Declassified*, NOVA/PBS special.

Page 111: "Wernher, I must . . . live." Medaris in Ward, 98.

Page 111: Von Braun's victory dance: ibid.

Chapter 16: Object D

Page 113: "1.3 tons": Siddiqi, *The Red Rockets' Glare*, 334.

Page 113: "What if we . . . simpler": Mikhail Tikhonravov quoted in ibid.

Page 113: one or two . . . source: ibid.

Page 114: no method . . . clarity in space: ibid., 338.

Page 114: Temperature fluctuations . . . meteorites: ibid.

Page 114: "Couldn't you make it . . . kind": ibid.

Page 115: "Tell him . . . won't": von Braun quoted in Ward, 99.

Chapter 17: Sputnik

Page 116: Weather described: Siddiqi, *The Red Rockets' Glare*, 350.

Page 117: Fifteen minutes before . . . personnel: ibid., 352.

Page 117: At the ten minute mark . . . liftoff: ibid.

Page 117: "instantly on the alert . . . on": Evgenii Shabarov, ibid., 353.

Page 117: "Ten minutes to readiness": voice over loudspeaker, ibid., 352.

Page 117: Translation of Russian countdown sequence: ibid., 353.

Page 117: "Contact liftoff!": ibid.

Page 117: "There was absolute . . . orbit": Mikhail Rebrov quoted in Harford, 129.

Page 118: Outside, Viacheslav Lappo . . . transmission: events of Sputnik launch, Siddiqi, *The Red Rockets' Glare*, 355.

Page 118: "It's there! . . . recorders": Lappo, 356.

Page 118: teary-eyed men: Harford, 129.

Page 118: "junior specialists . . . labor." Siddiqi, *The Red Rockets' Glare*, 356.

ENDNOTES

Chapter 18: *Bleep-Bleep-Bleep*

Page 120: "What do you . . . orbited": Robinson, "The Story behind the Explorers," *This Week Magazine*, April 13, 1958, 36.

Page 120: "We knew . . . days": von Braun quoted in Medaris, 155.

Page 121: "Ninety days"; "get the stuff . . . proceed": Medaris, 155, 157.

Page 121: "Come listen": Homer Hickam, *Rocket Boys*, chapter 2, ebook.

Page 121: "buttered toast"; "hot chocolate": ibid.

Page 121: He expected to hear rock and roll: ibid.

Page 121: "the tone . . . space": ibid.

Page 122: "What is this thing, Sonny?" ibid.

Page 122: "The bright little ball . . . it": ibid.

Page 123: "raise [his] apprensions . . . iota": Eisenhower, 123rd press conference, www.youtube.com/watch?v=fJBitwFULCU.

Chapter 19: The Invisible Man

Page 125: Valentin Glushko's . . . from official historical records: Siddiqi, *Sputnik and the Soviet Space Challenge*, 169.

Page 126: Six-column-wide . . . war: Brzezinksi, Matthew, *Red Moon Rising*, 171–172.

Page 126: Soviet fires . . . U.S.: *New York Times*, October 5, 1957, www.nytimes.com/partners/aol/special/sputnik/sput-01.html.

Page 126: Winter Is an Urgent Task: Siddiqi, *The Red Rockets' Glare*, 358.

Page 127: Korolev hesitated . . . time: Chertok, *Rockets and People: Creating a Rocket Industry*, Vol. 2, 387.

Chapter 20: Laika and the Cosmo-Mutt Cover-Up

Page 128: "thirteen-foot . . . instruments": NASA Space Science Data Coordinated Archive, www.nssdc.gsfc.nasa.gov/nmc/spacecraft/display .action?id=1957-002A.

Page 128: Dates and times of Laika's placement inside the satellite, weather conditions, and launch date: Siddiqi, *Sputnik and the Soviet Space Challenge*, 173–74.

Page 129: "Everyone was very concerned": Viktor Yazdovsky, "The Dog

That Orbited the Earth," BBC Witness History documentary.

Page 130: "They knew she . . . journey": ibid.

Page 130: "wanted to do . . . her": Vladimir Yazdovsky, ibid.

Page 130: Laika's death and subsequent cover-up: Anatoly Zak, "Laika Declassified," *Smithsonian Air & Space Magazine*, www .airspacemag.com/daily-planet/laika-declassified-180967077.

Page 131: "The Russians love . . . humanity": Latson, "The Sad Story of Laika, the First Dog Launched into Orbit."

Page 131: "the shaggiest, lonesomest, saddest dog in all history": Wellerstein, "Remembering Laika, Space Dog and Soviet Hero."

Chapter 21: The Invisible Woman

Page 134: The timing . . . hand: Object label, Saturn V Hall, *Explorer 1*, US Space & Rocket Center Museum, Huntsville, Alabama, visited by the author March, 4, 2019.

Page 134: "I had to wear . . . life": Joyce Neighbors, interview with the author, March 6, 2019.

Page 136: During the Jim Crow era . . . cafeterias: "Racial Relations: The Changing Role of Race at NASA Langley," https://crgis.ndc.nasa .gov/historic/Racial_Relations.

Page 136: "If she says they're good, then I'm ready to go": Katherine Johnson recalls John Glenn's words in Johnson, *Reaching for the Moon: The Autobiography of NASA Mathematician Katherine Johnson*, 209–210.

Chapter 22: The American Satellite

Page 137: a tremendous . . . smoke: "Poof! US Fires Dudnik," *Humboldt Standard*, Dec. 6, 1957, 1. Newspaperarchive.com, www.newspaperarchive .com/eureka-humboldt-standard-dec-06-1957-p-1/).

Page 138: The *Pravda* reprinting of the *London Daily Herald* described in Harford, 133.

Page 138: The Vanguard program . . . orbit: Vanguard 1 Satellite, 1958. Hollingham, "The World's Oldest Scientific Satellite Is Still in Orbit."

Page 139: Debus's denouncement of colleagues to the Gestapo discussed with Neufeld in telephone interview with the author, December 20, 2019.

Page 140: "seemed charged with electricity": Medaris, 219.

Page 140: "As the missile . . . voice"; "that sounded like . . . 'Go, baby, go!'"; "up and up. Faster and faster": ibid.

Page 141: Only a confirmation . . . achieved.: Medaris, 222, 224.

Page 141: Forty minutes later: ibid., 223.

Page 141: "I'm out of coffee . . . us.": ibid., 223.

Page 141: "I repeated . . . aloud": ibid., 225.

Page 141: From a nearby . . . satellite: ibid., 225.

Page 142: "We have firmly . . . again": Von Braun, quoted in *Time* magazine, February 17, 1958.

Page 143: "two donuts of seething radiation": Karen Fox, "NASA's Van Allen Probes Spot an Impenetrable Barrier in Space."

Page 143: Korolev's work with the translator described by Vladimir Shevalyov to Harford, 244.

Chapter 23: NASA Is Born

Page 147: "Their recent progress is . . . challenge": Wernher von Braun, *American Weekly*, August 3, 1958.

Chapter 24: "The Right Stuff"

Page 150: "Place a manned . . . safely": Project Mercury Overview: Objectives and Guidelines, www.nasa.gov/mission_pages/mercury/missions /objectives.html.

Page 151: "to go up . . . infinite": Wolfe, 17.

Page 152: "We were treated like a bunch of lab rats": L. Gordon Cooper and Bruce B. Henderson, *Leap of Faith*, 17.

Page 152: "The doctors got real creative . . . tests"; "Just when you thought . . . pad"; "We were probed . . . week": ibid.

Page 153: "These men . . . flight": Transcript, NASA Press Conference, Mercury Astronaut Team, April 9, 1959, www.nasa.gov/pdf/147556main _presscon.pdf.

Page 153: "Rarely were history's explorers . . . destiny": "The Seven

Chosen," *Time* magazine, Vol. LXXIII No. 16, April 20, 1959, 17.

Page 154: The air force . . . 1946: "Redstone and Atlas."

Page 154: "about a half a mile"; "The sight of the Atlas . . . Disney"; "Searchlights played . . . it"; "thin-skinned . . . steel balloon; "we watched it . . . sky"; "looked like a hydrogen bomb"; the astronauts ducked; "Well, I'm glad . . . way": Glenn, ebook, chapter 14.

Chapter 25: Squirrel and Little Arrow

Page 156: he seemed to like dogs . . . launches: Siddiqi, *Sputnik and the Soviet Space Challenge*, 252.

Page 157: Soviet scientists . . . weightlessness; became more animated . . . convulsions; struggling Belka vomited; sad sight . . . orbit: Siddiqi, *Sputnik and the Soviet Space Challenge*, 253.

Page 158: "was not as dramatic . . . well." Kennedy's letter quoted in Alison Gee, "Pushinka: A Cold War Puppy the Kennedys Loved," www.bbc.com/news/magazine-24837199.

Chapter 26: Growing Pains at NASA

Page 159: The Redstone . . . arc: Neal Thompson, *Light This Candle*, chapter 10, ebook.

Page 160: "get the nation moving again": Kennedy, quoted in "Campaign of 1960," www.jfklibrary.org/learn/about-jfk/jfk-in-history/campaign-of-1960.

Page 160: "We were inventing . . . along": Kranz, *Failure Is Not an Option*, 28.

Page 161: "a change in the . . . room.": ibid., 29.

Page 161: "precisely at zero . . . smoke"; "nothing on the screen but smoky sky.": ibid.

Chapter 27: Blast Radius

Page 162: "Over a period of . . . orbit": Chertok, *Rockets and People*, Vol. 2, 597.

Page 163: "Superstitious Russians . . . bad luck": Siddiqi explains that leap years are considered unlucky in Russia. See footnote in Chertok, *Rockets and People*, Vol. 2, 598.

Page 164: domineering personalities: Siddiqi, *Sputnik and the Soviet Space Challenge*, 112–113.

Page 164: Korolev preferred to . . . deputy: ibid. 113.

Page 164: The friendly rivalry between Korolev and Yangel as described by Siddiqi, in an email correspondence with the author, December 17, 2019.

Page 164: devil's venom: Hardesty and Eisman, 35.

Page 164: When it came to . . . Force: Chertok, *Rockets and People*, Vol. 2, 602.

Page 165: Yangel's political relationship with Nedelin and Khrushchev, Cadbury, 183.

Page 165: Mrykin and Yangel's cigarette break: Siddiqi, *Sputnik and the Soviet Space Challenge*, 256.

Page 165: five hundred feet from the launch site: Chertok, *Rockets and People*, Vol. 2, 618.

Page 165: fifty feet away: Michael T. Kezirian, PhD, Joseph Pelton, PhD, Tommaso Sgobba, "The Russian R-16 Nedelin Disaster: An Historical Analysis of Failed Safety Management," 69.

Page 165: "We'll modify the missile . . . us": Chertok recalls Nedelin's comments, *Rockets and People*, Vol. 2, 615.

Page 166: organ-dissolving chemicals: Mark Everest, Christopher Spencer, *Space Race*, episode 3, BBC, 2005.

Page 166: an electrical error . . . engine: Hardesty and Eisman, 35.

Page 166: The rocket's fuel tank detonated: ibid.

Page 166: Descriptions of Nedelin disaster victims: Kezirian, Pelton, and Sgobba, 69.

Page 167: Only a single . . . identity. Siddiqi, *Sputnik and the Soviet Space Challenge*, 258.

Page 167: an aircraft accident: ibid.

Page 167: Revelation of truth of Nedelin disaster: Siddiqi, telephone interview with the author, October 25, 2019.

Page 167: 126 people died: Siddiqi, *Sputnik and the Soviet Space*

Challenge, 258. In footnote 42 on this page, Siddiqi states that the number of deaths in the Nedelin disaster varies among sources.

Chapter 28: The First to Fly

Page 169: "You might think . . . back": Thompson, chapter 1.

Page 171: A valve malfunctioned . . . course: Thompson, chapter 13, ebook.

Page 172: he was livid: ibid.

Chapter 29: The Russians' "Right Stuff"

Page 173: Gagarin's reading of Hemingway in the Soviet medical center: Jenks, "The Russian Icarus: How Gagarin Became Cosmonaut #1."

Page 173: Soviet fascination with Ernest Hemingway: ibid.

Page 173: Scott, Leonov, Toomey, sat shirtless . . . turn: Gagarin described by Leonov: *Two Sides of the Moon*, Chapter 2, ebook.

Page 174: "Hello, my little eagles": Alexei Leonov quoted in *The Russian Right Stuff*: "The Invisible Spaceman," episode 1.

Page 174: "Hello!"; "He was looking . . . everything": ibid.

Page 174: "blue eyes . . . smile": Leonov quoted in Harford, 159.

Page 174: March 9, 1934, in the village of Klushino, a hundred miles from Moscow: Doran and Bizony, *Starman*, chapter 1.

Page 175: They seized the Gagarins' house; seek shelter . . . storage; Russians used . . . straw: Jenks, *The Cosmonaut Who Couldn't Stop Smiling: The Life and Legend of Yuri Gagarin*, 36, footnote 32.

Page 175: Suicide of Russian colonel recalled by Valentin Gagarin in Doran and Bizony, chapter 1, ebook.

Page 175: The Gagarin children's resistance activities: ibid.; Jenks, 38.

Page 176: Boris wept . . . bled; pointed his rifle; by an officer: Doran and Bizony, chapter 1, ebook.

Page 176: Using the scarf . . . camera: Jenks, 36, 37, footnote 33.

Page 176: The effects of torture on Boris Gagarin's ability to walk, ibid.

Page 176: shoved dirt . . . equipment: ibid., 38.

Page 177: "It was my fault . . . no one else is to blame": Valentin

ENDNOTES

Bondarenko quoted from Golovanov in Siddiqi, *Sputnik and the Soviet Space Challenge*, 266, see footnote 71.

Chapter 30: *"Poyekhali!"* ("Let's Go!")

Page 178: sixty-five beats per minute: Vladimir Yakovlevich Khilchenko quoted in John Rhea, ed., *Roads to Space*, 387.

Page 178: "Everything is normal . . . feel." Gagarin's Vostok 1 flight transcript excerpted and translated in Siddiqi, *Sputnik and the Soviet Space Challenge*, 277.

Page 178: "I feel excellent . . . well": ibid.

Page 179: "I see the clouds . . . beautiful": ibid.

Page 180: one hour and forty-eight minutes: ibid., 281.

Page 180: inside an unmarked car: ibid., 282.

Chapter 31: "Light This Candle"

Page 181: "It is a most . . . feat": John F. Kennedy quoted in news conference 9, April 12, 1961, www.jfklibrary.org/archives/other -resources/john-f-kennedy-press-conferences/news-conference-9.

Page 182: $40 billion: Hardesty and Eisman, 120.

Page 182: "Do we have a chance . . . win?": Kennedy in John Logsdon, ed., *The Penguin Book of Outer Space Exploration*, 158.

Page 183: "We have an excellent chance . . . 1967/68": ibid.

Page 184: The suit was . . . exertion: Thompson, chapter 14, ebook.

Page 185: for more than three hours: ibid.

Page 185: "Man, I got . . . myself": ibid.

Page 186: the urine was . . . space suit: ibid.

Page 186: "Why don't you . . . light this candle": ibid.

Page 186: Forty-five million Americans: NASA.gov, "US Human Spaceflight: A Record of Achievement, 1961–2006," www.history.nasa .gov/monograph41.pdf, 13.

Page 187: "These are extraordinary . . . cause"; "Now it is time . . . Earth"; "No single space . . . accomplish": JFK address to a joint session of Congress, May 25, 1961, 2017, www.youtube.com

/watch?v=TUXuV7XbZvU.

Page 187: von Braun . . . associates: Ward, 128.

Page 189: four hundred double-decker buses: *Equinox*, season 2, episode 1, "The Engines That Came in from the Cold," www.youtube .com/watch?v=BLg1QUq5GQM.

Page 189: estimated cost of manufacturing . . . rubles: Harford, 257.

Page 189: actual cost . . . four billion rubles: ibid.

Chapter 32: Behind the Wall

Page 192: "We felt like like wild . . . pounce": Peter Guba quoted in "The Berlin Wall," documentary video.

Page 193: powered through discomfort . . . pace: Siddiqi, *Sputnik and the Soviet Space Challenge*, 361.

Page 193: He obsessed . . . operation: ibid.

Page 193: intestinal bleeding . . . unbearable pain: ibid., footnote 32.

Chapter 33: "She Is a Gagarin in a Skirt"

Page 195: "You're working . . . space.": Siddiqi, "The First Woman in Earth Orbit," *Spaceflight* Vol. 51, January 2009, 20–21.

Page 195: "Everything is normal . . . arrangement"; "I am not a delicate lady": ibid., 21.

Page 196: as long as . . . air: Valentina Tereshkova quoted in Mary Dejevsky, "The First Woman in Space," Guardian.com.

Page 197: "was marvelous": ibid.

Page 197: four hundred women candidates: Siddiqi, *Sputnik and the Soviet Space Challenge*, 353.

Page 197: altitude of more than four miles: Libby Jackson, *Galaxy Girls*, 32.

Page 197: the selection . . . cosmonauts: Siddiqi, *Sputnik and the Soviet Space Challenge*, 246.

Page 197: "taking walks . . . son": Kamanin's journal quoted in ibid., 362.

Page 198: "We must first send Tereshkova . . . skirt": ibid.

Page 198: the Seagull reported . . . continue: Siddiqi, "The First

Woman in Earth Orbit," 22.

Page 198: just another . . . West: Siddiqi, *Sputnik and the Soviet Space Challenge*, 369.

Page 199: "Women of the world . . . success": Valentina Tereshkova's flight transcript quoted in Siddiqi, "The First Woman in Orbit," 24.

Page 199: all six American . . . combined: Siddiqi, *Sputnik and the Soviet Space Challenge*, 373.

Chapter 34: "The President Has Been Shot"

Page 200: Korolev lived . . . services: suspicion that his phone was tapped; Criticism of the Americans . . . circles; the chief designer felt . . . well.; Harford, 234.

Page 201: Admire the US: ibid.; "never heard Korolev criticize America.": Vladimir Shevalyov, ibid.

Page 202: "What a waste . . . leader": Bonnie Holmes recollections quoted in Ward, 132.

Page 202: it was the only . . . cry: ibid.

Page 202: "Like for so many . . . me": Wernher von Braun's letter to Mrs. Kennedy, exhibit, US Space & Rocket Center Museum, Huntsville, Alabama. Author visit March 7, 2019.

Page 202: "What a wonderful world . . . him." Mrs. Kennedy's letter to Wernher von Braun, ibid.

Chapter 35: Stepping Stones to the Moon

Page 205: "long-duration flight . . . moon": "Gemini: Bridge to the Moon."

Page 205: Korolev hoped . . . moon: Harford, 180.

Page 205: "launch of . . . away!": Vasily Mishin, ibid.

Page 206: Modifications of Vostok to accommodate additional cosmonauts for Voskhod missions: ibid., 181.

Page 207: F-1 engine functioning: *The Great Hope*, exhibit, US Space & Rocket Center Museum, Huntsville, Alabama, author visit March 7, 2019.

Page 208: one week later . . . attack.: Harford, 277.

Page 208: Most of the . . . systems: Siddiqi, email correspondence with the author, December 17, 2019.

Page 208: "The scope of . . . alarm": Korolev's letter quoted in Siddiqi, *Sputnik and the Soviet Space Challenge*, 405.

Page 208: "In this . . . Soviet Union": ibid.

Page 209: Voskhod 1 soft landing described: Sparrow et al., eds., *The Illustrated Encyclopedia of Space & Space Exploration*, 311.

Page 210: "It was taking far longer . . . to": Alexei Leonov, "The Nightmare of Voskhod 2."

Page 210: "My temperature . . . high"; "drenched with sweat, my heart racing"; "We had only . . . ammunition"; "as the sky . . . howl.": ibid.

Page 212: "saddest moment of my life": White quoted in Ben Evans, "'The Saddest Moment': The Story of America's First Space Walk," Part 2.

Page 213: planned to be . . . 1968: Cadbury, 285.

Page 214: fill a family-size . . . seconds: *Space Race*, episode 4, BBC, www.youtube.com/watch?v=wZI8uLCsjlU.

Page 215: Each of the five bell . . . Dams: "The Mighty F-1 Engine Powered the Saturn V Rocket," www.nasa.gov/centers/marshall/history /f1_engine_new.html.

Page 215: The human toll of the space race on the personal lives and health of those involved, as discussed with Homer Hickam in interview with the author, March 5, 2019.

Page 216: tired easily: Harford, 276.

Page 216: Antonina Zlotnikova's recollection of Korolev stating his plans to die at his desk, quoted from Alexander Ishlinksky in Harford, 277. See also note 367.

Page 216: "I am somehow unusually . . . bit": Korolev's letter to his wife, quoted in Harford, 276.

Page 217: American military advisers . . . 1965: Ronald H. Spector, "Vietnam: 1954–1975," Britannica.com., www.britannica.com/event /Vietnam-War.

Page 218: between 15,000 and . . . protesters: *Resistance and Revolution: The Anti-Vietnam War Movement at the University of Michigan, 1965–1972*,

"The March on Washington, www.michiganintheworld.history.lsa.umich
.edu/antivietnamwar/exhibits/show/exhibit/the_teach_ins/national_teach
_in_1965.

Page 218: it was the largest . . . history: ibid.

Chapter 36: *Da Svedaniya* ("Goodbye")

Page 220: "He was wearing . . . smile."; "run-down . . . thoughts.":
Chertok, *Rockets and People: Hot Days of the Cold War*, Vol. 3, 521.

Page 220: "Well, carry on!" Chertok recalls Korolev's last words to his
team: ibid.

Page 221: "less complicated than an appendectomy": ibid., 528.

Page 221: expected to return in one week: ibid.

Page 221: He was miserable.. . . Cosmodrome: Harford, 277.

Page 221: "I can't work like this any longer": Korolev's statement to his
wife, Nina Korolev, quoted from Golovanov in Harford, 276.

Page 222: "What are you doing?"; "It is hard enough to . . . him"; "there
is no way"; "Ministers come . . . business.": Mishin quoted from Tarasov in
Harford, 278.

Page 222: at eight a.m. . . . 1966: Harford, 279.

Page 222: "My father . . . operating table"; "cut the abdomen . . .
before.": Natalia Korolev in Harford, 279.

Page 222: the size of two fists: Golovanov quoted in Harford, 281.

Page 222: only had a few months to left to live; Thirty minutes after . . .
breathing: ibid.

Page 223: Doctors raced . . . him: ibid., 281.

Page 223: "It can't be this modest": Chertok, *Rockets and People*, Vol. 3,
530.

Page 223: "Korolev remained . . . persecution": ibid.

Page 224: "I was attempting . . . repression": ibid., 531.

Page 224: "Serbin frowned . . . lines": ibid.

Page 224: By nine a.m. . . . enter.: ibid., 539.

Page 224: "A particle of truth . . . them"; "There was a general sense . . .

secret"; "There was a shared . . . achievements": ibid., 540.

Page 225: "We wanted to be . . . us": ibid., 539.

Page 225: Korolev was cremated: ibid., 541.

Page 225: past Soviet leaders and heroes: Harford, 285.

Chapter 37: "A Rough Road Leads to the Stars"

Page 227: "If we die . . . life." Grissom quoted in Barbour, *Footprints on the Moon*, 125.

Page 228: "How are we . . . buildings": "The Apollo 1 Tragedy," NASA.gov, www.nssdc.gsfc.nasa.gov/planetary/lunar/apollo1info.html.

Page 228: "We've got a fire in the cockpit": Edward White, ibid.

Page 230: "three good friends" . . . stars: von Braun quoted in Ward, 139.

Page 230: bright, sunlit morning: Siddiqi, *The Soviet Space Race with Apollo*, 585.

Page 231: Power problems aboard Soyuz 1: Siddiqi, *The Soviet Space Race with Apollo*, 582–84.

Page 232: It was almost . . . a.m.: ibid., 585.

Page 232: suddenly the helicopter . . . side: ibid.

Page 232: Recollections of a rescue service member, ibid., footnote 68.

Page 232: resting on its side . . . fire: Soyuz 1 descent described by eyewitnesses in Siddiqi, *The Soviet Space Race with Apollo*, 587.

Page 232: Komarov had hit . . . crash: ibid., footnote 73.

Page 232: "We are very . . . cosmonauts": Astronauts' draft of telegram of condolence, NASA.gov, www.nasa.gov/pdf/743921main_Astronaut_condolence_telegram-Soyuz_1-%2024Apr1967.pdf.

Page 233: For years . . . accident: "Death of Yury Gagarin Demystified 40 Years On."

Chapter 38: Apollo Takes Flight

Page 235: "the question . . . sunk": "Apollo 4 and Saturn V," www.hq.nasa.gov/office/pao/History/SP-4205/ch9-5.html.

Page 235: "When that thing fired . . . throat.": Jim Jenkins, interview with the author, March 4, 2019.

ENDNOTES

Page 237: "We were like school kids . . . by": James Lovell, quoted in *NASA's Look at 50 Years of Apollo*, "Apollo 8: Around the Moon and Back," episode 3.

Page 238: "Suddenly I looked . . . moly": Frank Borman, ibid.

Page 238: "Oh, my God . . . pretty": Frank Borman, Apollo 8 Onboard Voice Transcription, NASA.gov, January 1969. http://historycollection.jsc .nasa.gov/JSCHistoryPortal/history/mission_trans/AS08_CM.PDF.

Page 238: "The vast loneliness . . . Earth"; "From the crew . . . Earth": James Lovell quoted in "Apollo Expeditions to the Moon," NASA.gov, www .history.nasa.gov/SP-350/ch-9-6.html.

Page 239: "disastrous": James Lovell quoted in Fairhead, *Mission Control: The Unsung Heroes of Apollo*, documentary film, Netflix.com.

Page 239: "To end the year . . . place": ibid.

Page 240: "What a place . . . painting,": Eugene Cernan, Apollo 10 Corrected Transcript, www.history.nasa.gov/afj/ap10fj/as10-day5-pt19.html.

Page 241: "I heard the thrusters . . . bang"; "We were fighter pilots . . . that"; a record-setting . . . hours; "We had all . . . feet.": Thomas Stafford quoted in *NASA's Look at 50 Years of Apollo*, episode 1, "Apollo 10," NASA, www.youtube.com/watch?v=Rq8cyvmJMNQ.

Page 241: Apollo 10 record: ibid.

Page 242: working twenty-four-hour . . . launch: *Equinox*, season 2, episode 1: "The Engines That Came in from the Cold."

Page 243: "In those first . . . victory": Boris Chertok: ibid.

Page 243: "sensitive to . . . objects": report quoted in Harford, 295.

Page 244: "Only he who does nothing . . . inadequate": Mishin quoted in Siddiqi, *The Soviet Space Race with Apollo*, 854.

Chapter 39: "One Small Step"

Page 246: an hour early: Watkins, *Apollo Moon Missions: The Unsung Heroes*, 8.

Page 246: monitor the lunar . . . computer: Fairhead.

Page 246: "probably more than . . . engineering": Steve Bales quoted in Watkins, 5.

Page 246: lit a cigarette; began reviewing his notes; could "cut it with a knife": ibid.

Page 247: "Program alarm"; "It's a 1202"; "We're GO on that alarm"; "Roger.": NASA Apollo 11 "Technical Air-to-Ground Voice Transmission, (GOSS NET 1) from the Apollo 11 mission."

Page 247: "Steve! It's on our little list!": Bales recalled Garman's words in, *Mission Control*.

Page 248: "Better remind them . . . moon": Gene quoted in Alan Shepard, Deke Slayton, and Jay Barbree, *Moon Shot*, chapter 19, ebook.

Page 249: crossed his fingers; "I swear to God . . . happen": Alexei Leonov quoted in "One giant . . . lie? Why so many people still think the moon landings were faked." Guardian.com.

Page 249: The Soviet newspaper . . . story: Stone and Andres, *Chasing the Moon*, 275.

Page 249: Only select . . . landing: Siddiqi, *The Soviet Space Race with Apollo*, 697.

Page 250: "The night of . . . minute": letter from Mrs. Margaret and Michael Jennings quoted in Hansen, *Dear Neil Armstrong*, 121.

Page 250: "I adore space . . . an astronaut": André von Hebra's letter quoted in Hansen, 132.

Page 250: "My parents . . . it": Marianne Madden's letter quoted in Hansen, 171.

Page 250: "to record . . . flight"; "My only son . . . up": Jerry Hammond's letter quoted in Hansen, 193.

Chapter 40: Return to Rocket City

Page 252: Huntsville leadership capitalizes on the moon landing: Laney, *German Rocketeers in the Heart of Dixie*, 1–3.

Page 253: Huntsville population figures: Laney, 2.

Page 254: Over five thousand . . . Courthouse: Bob Dunnavant, "Mars Landing Decision Near, Says Von Braun," July 25, 1969, *Decatur Daily*, 1.

Page 254: "That ride was as . . . space": ibid.

Page 254: "Now that man . . . continue": ibid., 5.

Page 255: "Houston, we've had a problem here": Lovell mission's corrected transcript and commentary in Woods et al., *Apollo Flight Journal*.

Chapter 41: Life After Apollo

Page 258: Dr. Wernher von Braun . . . DC: Ward, 182.

Page 258: "Dr. von Braun . . . citizens": ibid.

Page 259: a new fifteen-million-dollar . . . complex: ibid.

Page 259: "My friends, there was dancing . . . slippers": Wernher von Braun quoted in "Huntsville Parties Like It's 1969 to Celebrate Lunar Landing Anniversary," www.whnt.com/2019/07/19/huntsville-parties -like-its-1969-to-celebrate-lunar-landing-anniversary.

Page 259: conflicted feelings about going to Washington: Konrad Dannenberg quoted in Ward, 177.

Page 260: "I've found out . . . accent": John Goodrum, ibid., 197.

Page 262: shadow on his left kidney: Neufeld, *Von Braun*, 464.

Page 263: On August 22 . . . mass: ibid., 469.

Page 263: resist his doctor's orders . . . had: ibid., 464.

Page 263: less than an hour: ibid., 469.

Page 263: sedated during the last months . . . pain: ibid., 472.

Page 263: three a.m. on Thursday, June 16, 1977: ibid.

Chapter 42: Out of the Shadows

Page 267: "The men that he . . . callous": Eli Rosenbaum quoted in Laney, 153.

Page 268: Additional evidence . . . involvement: Laney, 154.

Page 268: Rudolph was present at the hanging . . . watch: Judy Feigin, "The Office of Special Investigations: Striving for Accountability in the Aftermath of the Holocaust," 333.

Page 268: "a form of terror": ibid.

Page 269: the statute of . . . expired: Laney, 160.

Chapter 43: All That Remains

Page 272: Name of SpaceX conference room "Von Braun": SpaceX tweet, March 23, 2015, www.twitter.com/spacex/status/5801589641904824 32?lang=en.

Author's Note

Page 277: "Wernher von Braun was . . . spaceflight?": Peenemünde Historical Technical Museum display, Peenemünde, Germany, visited by the author, April 7, 2019.

INDEX